COPENHAGEN

Like a Local

COPENHAGEN Like a Local

BY THE PEOPLE WHO CALL IT HOME

Contents

NIGHTLIFE

OUTDOORS

meet the locals

ALLAN MUTUKU KORTBÆK

After growing up in Denmark and Kenya, Allan made Copenhagen his home in 2009 and doesn't plan on leaving any time soon. A marketing creative, writer and photographer from 9 ' til 5, Allan spends his down-time by the water – swimming, surfing or running (if Tristan, his toddler, allows him to get a good night's sleep, that is).

MONICA STEFFENSEN

The co-founder of creative collective Merō, Monica has been photographing and writing about her city since 2014. When she's not working, you'll find her cycling between bakeries in search of Copenhagen's perfect cardamom bun, exploring the length and breadth of Denmark or jetting off to see the rest of the world.

Copenhagen

WELCOME TO THE CITY

You've heard it before: Denmark is one of the happiest places in the world. So, why are Copenhageners so happy? We'll let you into a little secret – it's not all about hygge. Few are quicker to challenge the status quo than Copenhageners. There's always room for improvement. And striving for the best means that they get the best – be it food, design or architecture. This is a place that's always looking forward and thinking about how to better itself, which might be why the Danish capital is on track to become the world's first carbon-neutral city.

If anywhere seems like a vision from the future it's Copenhagen. Beyond the oft-pictured terraces of Nyhavn, gleaming skyscrapers are made of sustainable, Lego-like blocks, scaled by climbing walls, ski slopes and vertical gardens. New Nordic chefs utilize the local environment by foraging for organic ingredients. And locals get around on super-fast bike paths and waterways clean enough to dive in (and people often do). That's not to say the past is forgotten. Folks are proud of Copenhagen's worn cobbled streets, crooked houses and stately palaces, highlights of the capital's long history that only seem to get better with age.

Understanding a city that is forever reinventing itself can feel like chasing a moving target. But that's where this book comes in. We know the places locals love best, from the swimming holes they brave in sub-zero temperatures to the street art they go out of their way to see. Of course, these pages can't capture every local's experience but instead offer a snapshot of the city.

Whether you're a restless local hungry to find the places that aren't on everyone else's radar, or you're a visitor wanting to rip up the traditional "to do" list, this book will help you embrace a different side to Copenhagen. Enjoy Copenhagen, the local way.

Liked by the locals

"Copenhagen sometimes feels like a slice of the liveable, green, sustainable future that we all dream of. It's always striving for better, without losing its humble heart."

ALLAN MUTUKU KORTBÆK,
WRITER, PHOTOGRAPHER AND
DIGITAL CONTENT SPECIALIST

Copenhagen takes on different personalities during each of the seasons. Think fun-filled festivals in summer and cosy, candlelit catch-ups in autumn.

Copenhagen THROUGH THE YEAR

SPRING

ALFRESCO DINING

As Copenhagen sheds its winter coat, locals don their shades and flock to pavement cafés for catch-ups over tasty tapas, classic smørrebrød and fresh oysters.

COPENHAGEN IN BLOOM

The short-lived cherry blossom season draws crowds outside to see the flowers bloom. Bispebjerg Cemetery and Sønderboulevard are particular favourites for a leafy stroll.

SAILING SEASON

The warmer months are welcomed by groups taking to the water in little boats, enjoying a singsong as they paddle.

SUMMER

OUTDOOR CINEMAS

As the evenings stretch out, locals hunker down at outdoor cinemas to enjoy films under the stars (blankets and bottles of wine are obligatory).

TO THE WATER

Whether it's a quick harbour dip during lunch hour or a family paddleboarding trip (dogs included), the water's the place to be when the mercury starts to soar.

DISTORTION FESTIVAL

Nothing brings music-loving locals together quite like this mammoth festival. For five days in June, thudding electronic music and outright hedonism fill the city streets.

THE GREAT ESCAPE

At the height of summer, when a dip in the harbour just doesn't cut it, Copenhageners flee the city in search of the nearest lake. Furesø is a favourite for long weekends.

AUTUMN

COSY CAFÉ VISITS

When Copenhagen's autumn storms begin, hygge is the perfect antidote. Locals gather in candlelit cafés to nurse cups of cocoa and while away the afternoons playing board games, all to the soundtrack of lashing rain.

KULTURNATTEN

For one night in October, culture is made free for all on Kulturnatten (Culture Night). Over 250 of the city's museums, theatres, libraries and churches throw open their doors for a range of fun exhibitions and concerts.

PARK VISITS

A break in the rain means a walk, a run or a cycle through the park. And though the city's greenery is much talked about, nothing beats the golden glow of fallen leaves here. For the best foliage, leaf-peepers head to the Botanical Gardens, Søndermarken or Frederiksberg Gardens.

WINTER

CHRISTMAS MARKETS

The sweet scents of *gløgg* (mulled wine) and roasted almonds waft through the air as folk wander through Copenhagen's warmly lit markets.

ICY DIP OR TOASTY TUB

While hardcore swimmers brave the icy waters during the winter, the rest of the city retreats to Copenhagen's many saunas or floating hot tubs to stay warm.

AMUSEMENT PARKS

Tivoli and Bakken become winter wonderlands during the dark months. Fairy lights adorn the parks' characterful streets and thrilling rides are illuminated against the night sky.

LET THERE BE LIGHT

Locals know how to beat the post-holiday blues – art. And in icy February, light installations spring up around the city, creating a huge outdoor gallery.

There's an art to being a Copenhagener, from the dos and don'ts of the bike lanes to negotiating the city's streets. Here's a breakdown of all you need to know.

Copenhagen KNOW-HOW

For a directory of health and safety resources, safe spaces and accessibility information, turn to page 190. For everything else, read on.

EAT

Copenhageners love their food (this is the hometown of superstar restaurant Noma after all) and tend to be early and punctual with their meals: breakfast kicks things off around 7am, lunch is served from 11:30am and dinner ticks in as early as 6pm. Most restaurants close for serving around 10pm, so don't turn up too late. Definitely book ahead to be sure of a spot, but there's rarely a need to dress up – unless you want to, of course.

DRINK

Coffee is taken seriously in this city, with locals savouring steaming lattes in *hyggelig* cafés and carrying takeaway cups wherever they go. Some coffee shops offer a discount if you bring a reusable cup.

Copenhagen has a reputation for being pricey and we're here to tell you the rumours are true: alcoholic drinks (especially cocktails) can be eye-wateringly expensive. To save money, do as the locals do – grab a drink from a supermarket and head to a park (it's legal to drink in public places here).

SHOP

Danish design is legendary and legendarily pricey. You can save 25 per cent by buying tax-free; just show your forms at the airport when you go home. To save money – and the environment – locals prefer to shop at flea markets and vintage stores. Shops are generally open from 9:30am to 5:30pm, though they often close earlier on weekends.

Markets are usually held on weekends only. Bear in mind that haggling isn't really the done thing. Oh, and it's always worth carrying a tote bag to avoid the charge for a plastic one.

ARTS & CULTURE

Culture comes at a price in Denmark's capital, with many museums charging €10–20. The good news is that a lot of places are free to enter on Tuesday. Theatre tickets are similarly pricey, but you can find deals online. The dress code is the same throughout Copenhagen: casual all the way.

NIGHTLIFE

There are two crowds when it comes to going out: those who hit the brown bars from as early as 7pm and those who party at home first before heading out around 12am. Most Copenhageners stay out till around 3 or 4am, when the clubs start to close. When it comes to what to wear, again, you don't need to dress up. Just be sure to have your ID on you – security at the door nearly always ask, however old you look.

OUTDOORS

Copenhageners congregate in parks and by the water at the slightest hint of sunshine. In the summer, don't be surprised if you see many topless or semi-nude locals working on their tan – it's a perfectly acceptable practice. There are recycling and rubbish bins wherever you go, so do your bit to help look after the city's green spaces.

Keep in mind

Here are some tips and tidbits that will help you fit in like a local.

» **Contactless** The majority of places take card – you can even use it at street food venues and on public transport.

» **No smoking** Lighting up is a no-no in most indoor spaces. Only a few brown bars allow people to smoke inside. If you do smoke, head to a designated spot outside.

» **Tipping** A tip of 5 to 10 per cent is the norm in restaurants, but there's no need to tip elsewhere.

» **Recycle your glass** Gather your glass bottles and return them to your nearest supermarket, where they're worth a few Kroner each.

GETTING AROUND

Copenhagen is shaped by water, laced by canals and split across the islands of Amager to the south and Zealand to the north. The city stretches out like the palm of the hand, with five built-up "fingers" separated by green spaces (no coincidence: the government's city expansion plan was titled the Fingerplanen). These fingers comprise ten administrative districts, each of which are home to a handful of neighbourhoods *(p14)*. Generally speaking, the locals think of Copenhagen in four distinct areas: Indre By (the central hub), north and west on the island of Zealand, and south on Amager.

To help you get around, we've provided what3words addresses for each sight in this book, meaning you can quickly pinpoint exactly where you're heading with ease.

On foot

Though cycling is the preferred mode of transport here, many locals choose to walk if distances are short. Besides which, walking is the best way to see the city in all its glory. Flat Indre By is very walkable, as are the neighbourhoods of Vesterbro and Frederiksberg, which have lovely leafy boulevards. Word of caution: locals are very fast walkers, so stick to one side of the pavement. And if you do need to stop and check your phone or a take a photo, step to the side so that people can pass.

On wheels

Copenhagen was made for cycling, with a fast and far-reaching network of cycle lanes. Be sure to familiarize yourself with the rules of the road and basic hand signals before you plunge into the blur of the bike lanes, where there can be up to eight lanes of fast-paced bike traffic. Keep to your right when you're cycling and never make a direct left turn at an intersection. If you move onto the pavement or a pedestrian crossing, always hop off your bike and walk. Helmets aren't legally required but most locals wear one, and we strongly advise you to do the same. Remember your lights at night (or risk a fine if the police stop you).

Bikes can be transported on S-trains (in the designated bike carriage at the start or end of the train) and on the metro any time outside of rush hour (7–9am and 3:30–5:30pm).

Bike rentals are available all over the city, with dedicated bike shops offering tours and short rentals *(p92)*. For longer trips, try Donkey Republic. ***www.donkey.bike***

By public transport

Copenhagen's S-trains connect the city centre with the suburbs. The modern metro also speeds through the city; it's open 24 hours a day, with a 2–4 minute wait between each train. Tickets for all public transport are easily available at stations or online – just make sure you save the ticket on your phone as parts of the metro can lack signal. When travelling up escalators, stand on the right if you don't want to walk up on the left (most locals walk).

Buses provide additional coverage and are in the process of being switched to 100 per cent electric power.

www.dsb.dk/en

www.intl.m.dk

By car or taxi

Driving in Copenhagen isn't recommended thanks to one-way streets and few parking spots. Indre By, in particular, is not car-friendly. Anyone brave enough to get behind the wheel should always be mindful of cyclists and pedestrians, who really rule the roads in this city. Mirror and blind spot checks are an absolute must.

Taxis are available in most parts of the city – look out for the green "Taxi" sign on top of the car and prepare to fork out a small fortune for a ride.

Download these

We recommend you download these apps to help you get about the city.

WHAT3WORDS

Your geocoding friend

A what3words address is a simple way to communicate any precise location on earth, using just three words. ///conned.risky.pocket, for example, is the code for *The Genetically Modified Little Mermaid* statue. Simply download the free what3words app, type a what3wordsaddress into the search bar, and you'll know exactly where to go.

REJSEPLANEN

Your local transport service

Rejseplanen's journey planning app lays out your best options for moving around the city (or anywhere in Denmark for that matter) and also provides links for purchasing tickets. All forms of transport are included in its easy-to-use interface, which is available to use on its website, too: *www.rejseplanen.dk*.

Copenhagen is a patchwork of neighbourhoods, each with its own character and community. Here we take a look at some of our favourites.

Copenhagen NEIGHBOURHOODS

Amager

When Copenhageners want to escape the city, they retreat to the island of Amager. Aside from its sprawling common and beach, Amager is home to CopenHill, the powerplant-turned-playground. *{map 6}*

Carlsberg Byen

The clue's in the name: this patch was home to Carlsberg 'til 2006. Today, the old brewery buildings house enviable apartments and world-class restaurants. *{map 2}*

Christianshavn

With its cobbled streets, tilting houses and canals, "Christian's Harbour" is a dead ringer for Amsterdam. On sunny days, locals come here to sit beside the water at alfresco bars and cafés, discussing current affairs and the latest exhibitions. *{map 5}*

Frederiksberg

Visitors flock to this stately municipality for the palace, gardens and tree-lined boulevards. Frederiksbergers stay on for the posh dining spots and top-notch shopping. {map 2}

Freetown Christiania

When hippies occupied this military compound in the 1970s, Freetown Christiania was anointed a haven for alternative living. Okay, it's seen its fair share of controversies over the years, including police raids of Pusher Street's cannabis market, but bohemian vibes live on at theatres, galleries and community centres. *{map 5}*

Hellerup

Only the wealthiest Copenhageners can afford to live in this aspirational, beachside suburb, but everyone dreams about being able to. Expect swanky mansions, sports cars, and bougie boutiques and bars. *{map 6}*

Indre By

Think of Copenhagen and you're probably picturing Indre By. The inner city is sprawling, encompassing everything from Nyhavn to

Strøget, Tivoli to *The Little Mermaid*. Locals come here on a daily basis to work and run errands, yes, but also to unwind. *{map 1}*

Klampenborg

Quiet during the week, this affluent area comes alive at the weekend, when families and friends flock to the beach or to enjoy a day of thrills at Bakken theme park. *{map 6}*

Kødbyen

A gritty centre for meat processing until the early 2000s, the Meatpacking District is now a hipster hub. Old slaughterhouses host uber-cool clubs, art galleries and restaurants. *{map 2}*

Latiner-kvarteret

Cool cafés, flea markets and bookshops galore (not to mention Copenhagen University's campus) make the Latin Quarter the city's student heartland. *{map 1}*

Nordhavn

Once a centre of industry, Nordhavn is now the poster child for sustainable urban development, with crowds of coffee-clutching creatives calling its modern, water-front apartments home. *{map 6}*

Nordvest

Fast replacing Nørrebro as the city's hipster enclave, Nordvest is awash with craft breweries, artisan coffee roasters and innovative start-ups. *{map 6}*

Nørrebro

Historically a multiethnic area, Nørrebro has seen contentious gentrification. Having said that, it's still hard to beat for powerful street art, global grub and buzzing bars. *{map 3}*

Østerbro

You know you're in Østerbro when you can see green for days. Copenhagen's largest park lies here – a city-centre escape where locals come to stretch their legs or read on the grass. *{map 3}*

Refshaleøen

This hipster hub is a local icon. Copenhageners might not live here but they regularly check out Refshaleøen's offbeat galleries, hop between stalls at the street food market and sip beers overlooking Indre By. *{map 4}*

Sydhavnen

Sydhavnen is a study in contrasts: long-time, working-class residents live side by side with hipsters, luxury flats neighbour tattered factories and old warehouses are trans-formed into forward-thinking community centres. *{map 6}*

Valby

A stone's throw from trendy Vesterbro – on the other side of Vestre Kirkegård – is sleepy Valby. The area flies under the radar despite its cool cafés and lovely green spaces. *{map 6}*

Vesterbro

Sex shops hark back to Vesterbro's history as Copenhagen's red-light district but today it's better known for its hip boutiques, family-friendly cafés and lively nightlife. *{map 2}*

Copenhagen

ON THE MAP

Whether you're looking for your new favourite spot or want to check out what each part of Copenhagen has to offer, our maps – along with handy map references throughout the book – have you covered.

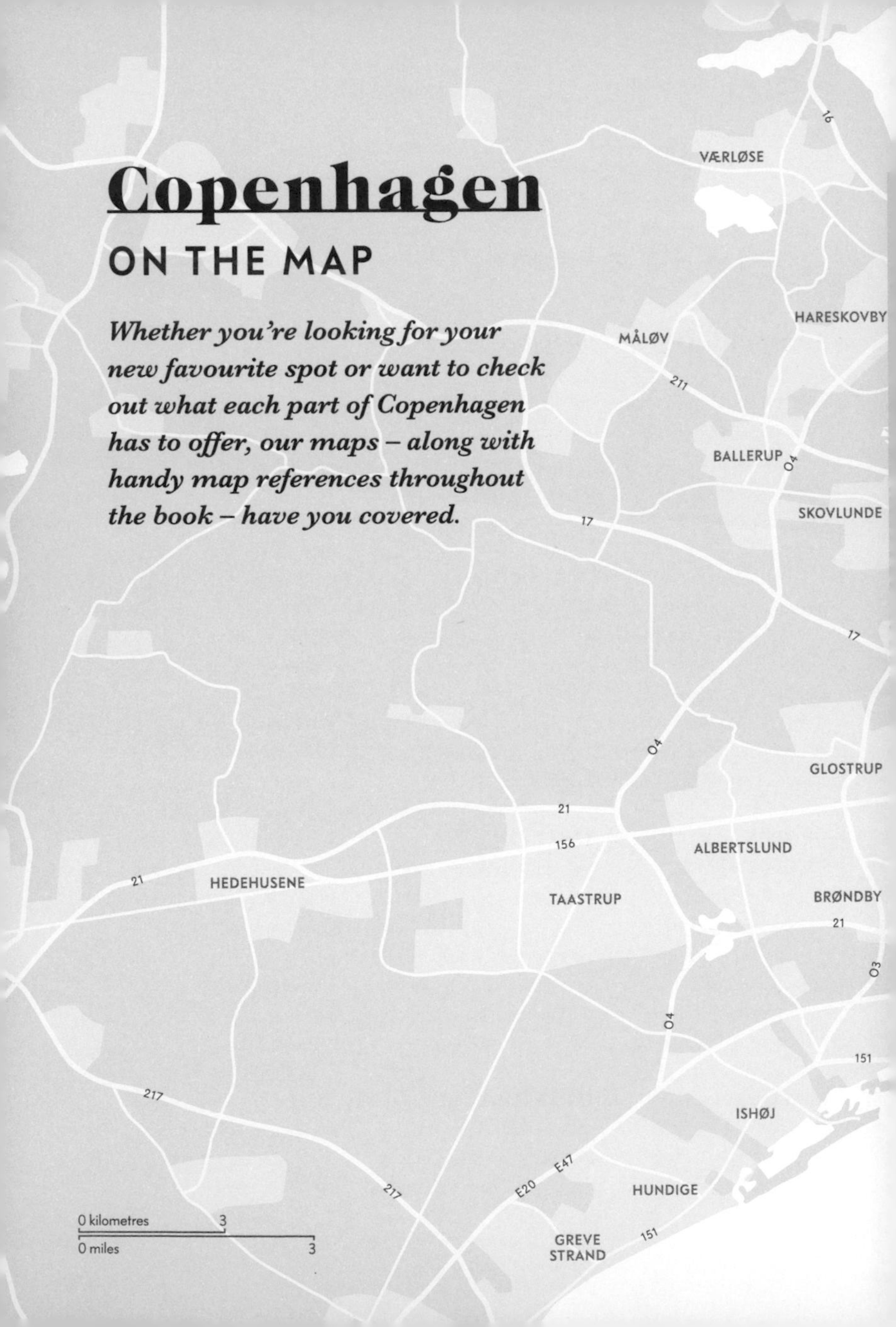
VÆRLØSE
16
HARESKOVBY
MÅLØV
211
BALLERUP
O4
SKOVLUNDE
17
17
O4
GLOSTRUP
21
156
ALBERTSLUND
21
HEDEHUSENE
TAASTRUP
BRØNDBY
21
O3
O4
151
ISHØJ
217
E47
E20
217
HUNDIGE
151
GREVE STRAND
0 kilometres
3
0 miles
3

VIRUM
Furesø
HJORTEKÆR
KONGENS LYNGBY
ORDRUP
BAGSVÆRD
JÆGERSBORG
Øresund
HELLERUP
SØBORG
HERLEV
EMDRUP
NØRDHAVN
ISLEV
BRØNSHØJ
ØSTERBRO
NØRREBRO
VANLØSE
FREDERICKSBERG
VESTERBRO
AMAGER
VALBY
HVIDOVRE
KASTRUP
TÅRNBY
Københavns Lufthavn
VIBERUP
DRAGOR
Køge Bugt
1
2
3
4
5
6

ÅBENRÅ
GOTHERSGADE
Restaurant Schønnemann
ISRAELS PLADS
NØRRE VOLDGADE
KULTORVET
VOGNMAGERG.
Cafe Hvide Lam
Melô
Cinnober Bookshop
FIOLSTRÆDE
NØRREGADE
Beat Bop
Folketeatret
DØP
Times Up Vintage
Ørstedsparken
LATINER-KVARTERET
Bo-bi Bar
Studenterhuset's Loppemarked
Le Fix
Democratic Coffee
KRYSTALGADE
KØBMAGERGADE
Café Paludan
Yonobi
LØVSTR.
The Jane
Paustian
GRÅBRØDRE-TORV
Gråbrødretorv
Balderdas
TEGLGÅRDSSTRÆDE
FRUE PLADS
SKT PEDERS STRÆDE
INDRE BY
KLOSTERSTRÆDE
SKINDERGADE
Naked
Never Mind Bar
Jailhouse CPH
Illums Bolighus
Charlie Scott's Bar
VIMMELSKAFTET
AMAGERTO
København K Charity Shop
Cosy Bar
VESTER VOLDGADE
STUDIESTRÆDE
Ecouture
BADSTUESTR.
HYSKENSTR.
NYGADE
Cafe Gammeltorv
LÆDERSTR.
NYTORV
BROLÆGGERSTR.
GAMMEL STRAN
Antik K
G*A*Y Copenhagen
VESTERGADE
FREDERIKSBERGGADE (STRØGET)
La Fontaine
Boghallen
Sonny
Centralhjørnet
RÅDHUSSTR.
VINDEBROGADE
NYBROGADE
HANS CHRISTIAN ANDERSENS BOULEVARD
LAVENDELSTR.
Taphouse
RÅDHUS-PLADSEN
FARVERGADE
Zefside
LØNGANGSTRÆDE
Stormbroen
VESTERBROGADE
Club Mambo
STORMGADE
Marmorbroen
National Museet
TØJHUSG
NY VESTERGADE
FREDERIKSHOLMS KANAL
Prinsensbro
VESTER VOLDGADE
TIETGENSGADE
Tivoli
DANTES PLADS
0 metres 200
0 yards 200
TIETGENSGADE

E EAT

Cafe Gammeltorv *(p43)*
DØP *(p46)*
Møntergade *(p40)*
Restaurant Schønnemann *(p41)*

D DRINK

Balderdash *(p75)*
Democratic Coffee *(p62)*
ILLUM Rooftop *(p65)*
Melô *(p68)*
Sonny *(p61)*
Taphouse *(p79)*
Ved Stranden 10 *(p69)*

S SHOP

Antik K *(p85)*
Beat Bop *(p107)*
Bike Copenhagen *(p92)*
Boghallen *(p102)*
Café Paludan *(p100)*
Cinnober Bookshop *(p102)*
Ecouture *(p96)*
Ganni *(p96)*
Hay House *(p90)*
Illums Bolighus *(p89)*
København K Charity Shop *(p87)*
Le Fix *(p99)*
Maria Black *(p98)*
Naked *(p98)*
Paustian *(p91)*
Studenterhuset's Loppemarked *(p84)*
Times Up Vintage *(p85)*
Yonobi *(p88)*

A ARTS & CULTURE

Folketeatret *(p121)*
National Museet *(p119)*
Nikolaj Kunsthal *(p126)*

N NIGHTLIFE

Bo-bi Bar *(p147)*
Cafe Hvide Lam *(p159)*
Centralhjørnet *(p152)*
Charlie Scott's Bar *(p159)*
Club Mambo *(p142)*
Cosy Bar *(p154)*
G*A*Y Copenhagen *(p153)*
Jailhouse CPH *(p153)*
The Jane *(p140)*
La Fontaine *(p156)*
Never Mind Bar *(p154)*
Zefside *(p141)*

O OUTDOORS

Gråbrødretorv *(p175)*
Ørstedsparken *(p165)*

THORVALDSENSVEJ
Landbohøjskolens Have
JULIUS THOMSENS PLADS
SKT MARKUS ALLE
Jørgens Sø
FREDERIKSBERG
DANASVEJ
BÜLOWSVEJ
H. C. ØRSTEDS VEJ
GRUNDTVIGSVEJ
KASTANIEVEJ
NIELS EBBESENS VEJ
VODROFFSVEJ
SVINERYGGEN
Sankt
FORHÅBNINGSHOLMS ALLE
GAMMEL KONGEVEJ
HOLLÆNDERVEJ
Sans Souci
AMICISVEJ
MADVIGS ALLÉ
Hart Bageri
Sound Station
Meyers Deli
Moseholm Yoga
Betty Nansen Teatret
FREDERIKSBERG ALLÉ
VÆRNEDAMSVEJ
Hanzō
Thiemers Magasin
GAMMEL KONGEV
Lidkoeb
FRYDENDALSVEJ
HENRIK IBSENS VEJ
Westend
Prag
VESTERBRO-TORV
Vela Gay C
Vinbaren Vesterbro Torv
VESTERBROGADE
VALDEMARSGADE
SAXOGADE
WESTEND
Gorda
Jojo Vesterbro
Brass Monkey
ISTEDGA
VESTERBROGADE
Designer Zoo
DANSK madeforrooms
MATTHÆUS-GADE
RAHBEKS ALLÉ
VESTERBRO
ENGHAVEVEJ
Sort Kaffe & Vinyl
Tomr Burger
Hooked
Mc. Kluud
ISTEDGADE
Prolog Coffee Bar
LYRSKOVGADE
Vega
Sidewalk SkateShop
Litauens Plads
Mesteren Lærlinge
SØNDER BOULEVARD
Café Sommersted
Enghave-parken
Enghave Plads
Dorma 21
NY CARLSBERG VEJ
Bageriet Brød
Beat
Mad & Kaffe
SKELBÆK-GADE
Cafe Dyrehaven
DYBBØLSGADE
NY CARLSBERG VEJ
CARLSBERG BYEN
VESTERFÆLLEDVEJ
Folkehuset Absalon
ENGHAVEVEJ
SØNDER BOULEVARD
Baisikeli
INGERSLEVSGADE
Vores Vinbar
Vang & Bar
0 metres 300
0 yards 300

E EAT

Bageriet Brød *(p36)*
Cafe Dyrehaven *(p40)*
Folkehuset Absalon *(p44)*
Gorda *(p48)*
Hunzo *(p46)*
Hart Bageri *(p38)*
Hooked *(p45)*
Mad & Kaffe *(p33)*
MASH Penthouse *(p52)*
Meyers Deli *(p35)*
Sans Souci *(p41)*
Tommi's Burger Joint *(p50)*

D DRINK

Brass Monkey *(p75)*
Jojo Vesterbro *(p72)*
Lidkoeb *(p75)*
Prolog Coffee Bar *(p60)*
Vang & Bar *(p73)*
Vinbaren Vesterbro Torv *(p69)*
Vores Vinbar *(p70)*
WarPigs *(p77)*

S SHOP

Baisikeli *(p93)*
Beat *(p104)*
DANSK madeforrooms *(p89)*
Designer Zoo *(p90)*
Dorma 21 *(p107)*
Prag *(p87)*
Sidewalk SkateShop *(p97)*
Sort Kaffe & Vinyl *(p104)*
Sound Station *(p105)*
Thiemers Magasin *(p102)*

A ARTS & CULTURE

Betty Nansen Teatret *(p120)*
Cykelslangen *(p129)*
Warehouse9 *(p122)*
Westend *(p132)*

N NIGHTLIFE

Bremen *(p143)*
Café Sommersted *(p147)*
Jolene Bar *(p141)*
Mc. Kluud *(p145)*
Mesteren & Lærlingen *(p140)*
Pumpehuset *(p151)*
Vega *(p149)*
Vela Gay Club *(p152)*

O OUTDOORS

Enghave Plads *(p175)*
Landbohøjskolens Have *(p167)*
Litauens Plads *(p172)*
Moseholm Yoga *(p179)*

0 metres 400
0 yards 400
LERSØ
HARALDSGADE
PARKALLÉ
ALDERSROGADE
JAGTVEJ
SERRIDSLEVVEJ
Teater Republique
VERMUNDSGADE
TAGENSVEJ
SIGURDSGADE
ØSTER ALLÉ
NØRRE ALLÉ
JAGTVEJ
Superkilen Park
BaNanna Park
MIMERSGADE
Københavns Universitet
Fælled-parken
FREDERIK V'S VEJ
TAGENSVEJ
NØRREBROGADE
GULDBERGS PLADS
FENSMARKGADE
JAGTVEJ
SJÆLLANDSGADE
JULIANE MARIES VEJ
BLEGDAMSVEJ
Mikkeller & Friends
Second Beat Antikvariat
RYESGADE
NØRRE ALLÉ
Amor-parken
NØRREBRO
Terroiristen
Crate – Beer & Vinyl
NØRREBROGADE
MØLLEGADE
FREDENSGADE
Mirabelle
BÆST
Brus
Res-Res
Ark Books
Rust
JAGTVEJ
Assistens Kirkegård
BLEGDAMSVEJ
RYESGADE
Fredens Bro
Pompette
SKT HANS TORV
Andersen & Maillard
DOSSERING
Sortedams Sø
ELMEGADE
Galleri KBH Kunst
Kind of Blue
Route 66
SORTEDAM
ØSTER SØGADE
RANTZAUSGADE
KAPELVEJ
STENGADE
Bevar's
ØSTER FARIMAGSGADE
Kølsters Tolv Haner
Sasaa
Props Coffee Shop
Depanneur
Tjilli Pop
Fødder Mødes
Blågårds Plads
Dronning Louises Bro
SØTORVET
Københavns Cykelbørs
ÅGADE
Botanisk Have
DOSSERING
Slurp Ramen Joint
ARK
KORSGADE
ÅBOULEVARD
Café Vélo
Funchs Vinstue
Stilleben
ÅBOULEVARD
WORSAAESVEJ
PEBLINGE
Peblinge Sø
NØRRE SØGADE
NØRRE FARIMAGSGADE
ISRAELS PLADS
NØRRE VOLDGADE
ROSENØRNS ALLÉ
JULIUS THOMSENS GADE
BÜLOWSVEJ
Ørsteds Parken

E EAT

Aamanns Deli & Takeaway *(p43)*
ARK *(p55)*
BÆST *(p50)*
Café Livingstone *(p35)*
Depanneur *(p46)*
Mirabelle *(p38)*
Sasua *(p47)*
Slurp Ramen Joint *(p49)*

D DRINK

Anderson & Maillard *(p61)*
Brus *(p79)*
Café Det Vide Hus *(p62)*
Kølsters Tolv Haner *(p76)*
Mikkeller & Friends *(p79)*
Terroiristen *(p68)*
Pompette *(p71)*
Props Coffee Shop *(p60)*

S SHOP

Ark Books *(p101)*
Café Vélo *(p93)*
Crate – Beer & Vinyl *(p105)*
Edie *(p86)*
I Blame Lulu *(p84)*
Københavns Cykelbørs *(p94)*
Res-Res *(p99)*
Route 66 *(p106)*
Second Beat Antikvariat *(p106)*
Stilleben *(p90)*

A ARTS & CULTURE

Assistens Kirkegård *(p112)*
BaNanna Park *(p132)*
Fødder Mødes *(p135)*
Galleri KBH Kunst *(p125)*
Statens Museum for Kunst *(p117)*
Teater Republique *(p123)*

N NIGHTLIFE

Bevar's *(p159)*
Funchs Vinstue *(p147)*
Kind of Blue *(p148)*
Rust *(p142)*
Tjilli Pop *(p151)*

O OUTDOORS

Blågårds Plads *(p173)*
Botanisk Have *(p164)*
Kongens Have *(p167)*
Søerne *(p169)*
Superkilen Park *(p172)*

0 metres
400
0 yards
400
ØSTERBRO
STRANDBOULEVARDEN
KALKBRÆNDERIHAVNSGADE
AMERIKA PLADS
The Genetically Modified Little Mermaid
CLASSENSGADE
KASTELSVEJ
FRIDTJOF NANSENS PLADS
REFSHALEØE
Garnisons Kirkegård
INDIAKAJ
KRISTIANIAGADE
FOLKE BERNADOTTES ALLÉ
Halvandet
Copenhag
Contempor
Baghaven
Reffen – Copenhagen Street Food
OSLO PLADS
Pedalatleten
Kastellet
Søndre Refshalebassin
bak
Østre Anlæg
GRØNNINGEN
La Banchina
RIGENSGADE
KRONPRINSESSEGADE
Nyboders Mindestuer
ESPLANADEN
SØLVGADE
BORGERGADE
Design Museum Danmark
Klint
LARSENS PLADS
Inderhavnen
Culture Box
AMALIEGADE
HOLMEN
Minebåds graven
Kongens Have
District Tonkin
BREDGADE
Amalienborg
Noma
Tranquebar
Jazzhus Montmartre
Lot#29
Martin Asbæk Gallery
Operaen
DANNESKIOLD - SAMSØES ALLÉ
Luftkastellet
TAPS Winebar CPH
Palæ
Sankt Annæ Plads
Ofelia Plads
KONGENS NYTORV
NYHAVN
Erdkehlgraven
REFSHALEVEJ
Móshù Cocktail Club
Skuespilhuset
Llama
Brønnum
Bådteatret
Det Kongelige Teater
DFDS Canal Tour
INDRE BY
Den Vandrette Winebar
Lykkemuseet
Cafe Malmø
HOLMENS KANAL
HAVNEGADE
PRINSESSEGADE

E EAT

District Tonkin *(p44)*

Klint *(p43)*

lille bakery *(p38)*

Llama *(p54)*

Noma *(p54)*

Reffen – Copenhagen Street Food *(p48)*

D DRINK

Baghaven *(p76)*

Brønnum *(p72)*

Den Vandrette Winebar *(p64)*

Halvandet *(p67)*

La Banchina *(p65)*

Luftkastellet *(p67)*

Móshù Cocktail Club *(p73)*

TAPS Winebar CPH *(p70)*

S SHOP

Lot#29 *(p97)*

Pedalatleten *(p94)*

Tranquebar *(p100)*

A ARTS & CULTURE

Amalienborg *(p113)*

Bådteatret *(p122)*

Copenhagen Contemporary *(p126)*

CopenHill *(p129)*

Design Museum Danmark *(p119)*

Det Kongelige Teater *(p120)*

The Genetically Modified Little Mermaid *(p135)*

Lykkemuseet *(p114)*

Martin Asbæk Gallery *(p124)*

Nyboders Mindestuer *(p115)*

Operaen *(p130)*

Skuespilhuset *(p131)*

N NIGHTLIFE

Cafe Malmø *(p145)*

Culture Box *(p142)*

Jazzhus Montmartre *(p157)*

Palæ *(p157)*

O OUTDOORS

DFDS Canal Tour *(p177)*

Kastellet *(p171)*

Ofelia Plads *(p174)*

Sankt Annæ Plads *(p174)*

Søndre Refshalebassin *(p181)*

INDRE BY
NYTORV
Inderhavnsbroen
Broens Gadekøkken E
Nærvær D
HOLMENS KANAL
CHRISTIANSBORG SLOTSPLADS
RÅDHUS-PLADSEN
Kayak Bar D
O GreenKayak
Dansk Jødisk Museum A
CHRISTIANS BRYGGE
Inderhavnen
TORVEGADE
Eiffel Bar N
The Great Story of the Little People and the Giant Trolls
Freetown Christiania A
Blue House Sandwich E
No. 2 E
A Prinsessegade
Vestergaard Møbler S
H. C. ANDERSENS BOULEVARD
VESTER VOLDGADE
FREDERIKSHOLMS KANAL
Tivoli
Ny Carlsberg Glyptoteket A
Blox A
Bryghusbroen
Lille Langebro
TIETGENSGADE
BERNSTORFFSGADE
CHRISTIANSHAVN
LANGEBROGADE
Langebro
Kalvebod Bølge O
O Go Boat
O Havneparken
Stadsgraven
AMAGER BOULEVARD
CHRISTMAS MØLLERS PLADS
VED STADSGRAVEN
AMAGER BLVD
Green Island of Copenhagen D
Kayak Polo O
WeCycle S
E Andersen Bakery
KALVEBOD BRYGGE
NJALSGADE
SVEND AUKENS PLADS
ISLANDS BRYGGE
HALFDANSGADE
Sydhavnen
STURLASGADE
ARTILLERIVEJ
NJALSGADE
AMAGERFÆLLEDVEJ
NORGESGADE
HAVNESTADEN
ØRESTADS BOULEVARD
Københavns Universitet
A Tietgenkollegiet
Brygge-broen
ARTILLERIVEJ
ISLANDS BRYGGE
E Far's Dreng
GRØNJORDSVEJ
O Havnevigen
O Amagerfælled
Grønjordssøen
ØRESTADS BOULEVARD
RØDE MELLEMVEJ
0 metres 500
0 yards 500

5

Ⓔ EAT

Amager Kebab 2001 *(p47)*
Andersen Bakery *(p37)*
Blue House Sandwich *(p45)*
Broens Gadekøkken *(p49)*
Far's Dreng *(p32)*
No. 2 *(p52)*

Ⓓ DRINK

Green Island of Copenhagen *(p64)*
Kayak Bar *(p67)*
Nærvær *(p71)*

Ⓢ SHOP

Christiania Cykler *(p92)*
Vestergaard Møbler *(p89)*
WeCycle *(p94)*

Ⓐ ARTS & CULTURE

Blox *(p128)*
Bøssehuset *(p123)*
Dansk Jødisk Museum *(p114)*
Freetown Christiania *(p115, p134)*
The Great Story of the Little People and the Giant Trolls *(p134)*
Ny Carlsberg Glyptoteket *(p117)*
Prinsessegade *(p133)*
Tietgenkollegiet *(p130)*

Ⓝ NIGHTLIFE

Café Nemoland *(p151)*
Christiania Jazz Club *(p157)*
Eiffel Bar *(p144)*
Jaguar Bodega *(p144)*
Operaen Christiania *(p148)*

Ⓞ OUTDOORS

Amagerfælled *(p167)*
Go Boat *(p179)*
GreenKayak *(p176)*
Havneparken *(p171)*
Havnevigen *(p182)*
Kalvebod Bølge *(p181)*
Kayak Polo *(p176)*

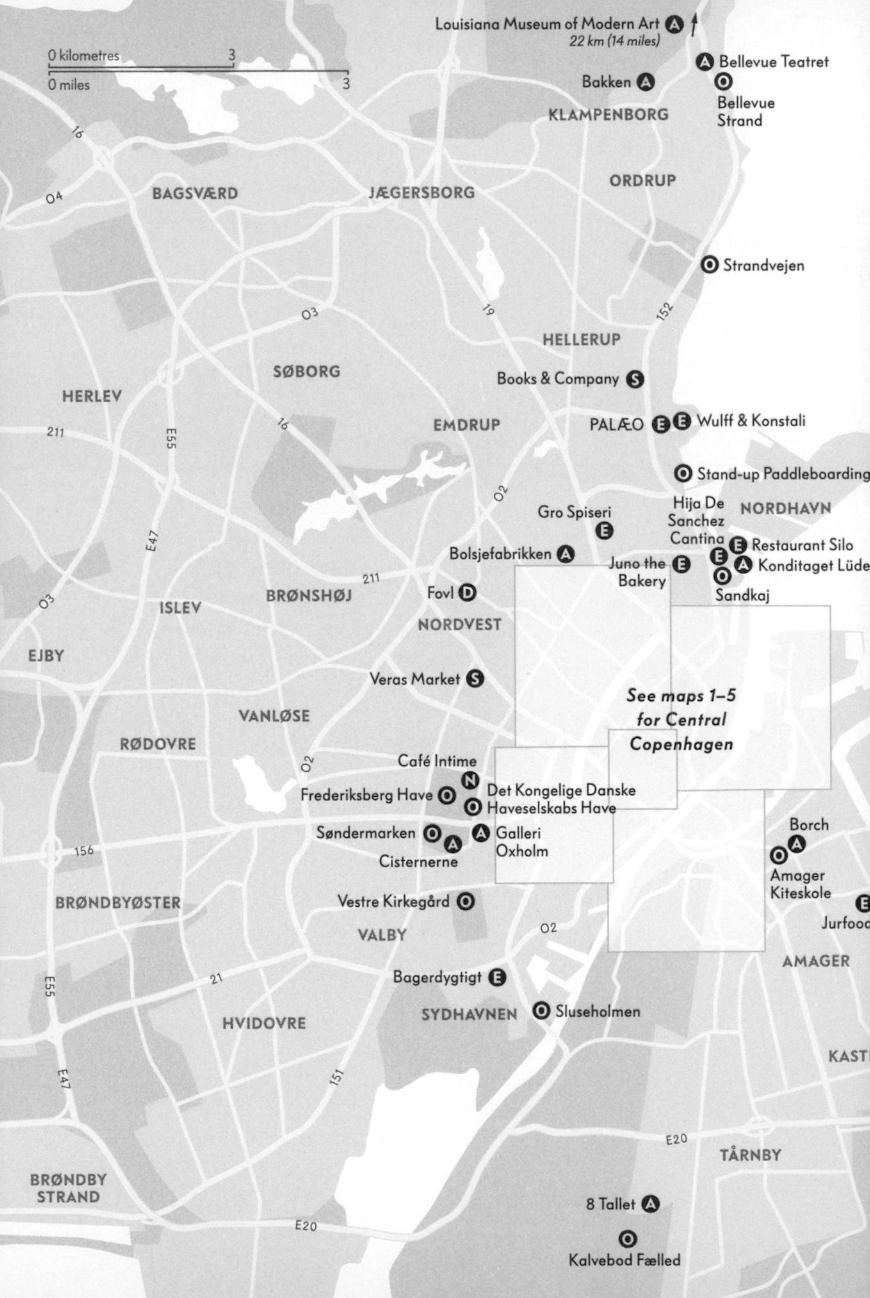

Louisiana Museum of Modern Art A
22 km (14 miles)
0 kilometres 3
0 miles 3
A Bellevue Teatret
Bakken A
O Bellevue Strand
KLAMPENBORG
ORDRUP
BAGSVÆRD
JÆGERSBORG
O Strandvejen
HELLERUP
SØBORG
Books & Company S
HERLEV
EMDRUP
PALÆO E
E Wulff & Konstali
O Stand-up Paddleboarding
Gro Spiseri E
Hija De Sanchez Cantina E
NORDHAVN
E Restaurant Silo
Bolsjefabrikken A
Juno the Bakery E
A Konditaget Lüder
O Sandkaj
BRØNSHØJ
Fovl D
ISLEV
NORDVEST
EJBY
Veras Market S
See maps 1–5 for Central Copenhagen
VANLØSE
RØDOVRE
Café Intime N
Frederiksberg Have O
Det Kongelige Danske Haveselskabs Have O
Søndermarken O
A Cisterne
A Galleri Oxholm
Borch A
O Amager Kiteskole
E Jurfood
BRØNDBYØSTER
Vestre Kirkegård O
VALBY
AMAGER
Bagerdygtigt E
SYDHAVNEN
O Sluseholmen
HVIDOVRE
KASTR
TÅRNBY
BRØNDBY STRAND
8 Tallet A
O Kalvebod Fælled

6

Øresund

Amager Strandpark

Københavns Lufthavn

E EAT

Bagerdygtigt *(p37)*

Gro Spiseri *(p53)*

Hija De Sanchez Cantina *(p50)*

Juno the Bakery *(p36)*

Jurfood *(p32)*

PALÆO *(p35)*

Restaurant Silo *(p55)*

Wulff & Konstali *(p33)*

D DRINK

Fovl *(p62)*

S SHOP

Books & Company *(p101)*

Veras Market *(p86)*

A ARTS & CULTURE

8 Tallet *(p130)*

Bakken *(p112)*

Bellevue Teatret *(p121)*

Bolsjefabrikken *(p134)*

Borch *(p124)*

Cisternerne *(p119)*

Galleri Oxholm *(p126)*

Konditaget Lüders *(p131)*

Louisiana Museum of Modern Art *(p116)*

N NIGHTLIFE

Café Intime *(p154)*

O OUTDOORS

Amager Kiteskole *(p179)*

Amager Strandpark *(p182)*

Bellevue Strand *(p180)*

Det Kongelige Danske Haveselskabs Have *(p165)*

Frederiksberg Have *(p164)*

Kalvebod Fælled *(p169)*

Sandkaj *(p182)*

Sluseholmen *(p180)*

Søndermarken *(p168)*

Strandvejen *(p171)*

Stand-up Paddleboarding *(p177)*

Vestre Kirkegård *(p168)*

EAT

Copenhageners love to get creative with food. Chefs reimagine classic dishes and bakes, and celebrate foraged ingredients. The result? An ever-evolving food scene.

Brunch Spots

Popular with carb-seeking students and young families on weekend jaunts, brunch is a low-key affair in Copenhagen – though in true Danish style, understated means anything but ordinary.

FAR'S DRENG

Map 5; Islands Brygge 79a, Islands Brygge; ///impaired.protect.cracker; www.farsdreng.com

Come the weekend, groups of friends congregate at this waterfront spot to nurse strong cups of coffee and atone for the actions of the night before. Run by a father and son duo, it's the kind of place that really knows its audience: check out the so-called "breakfast hangover burger" on the menu. If you're not in dire need of a pick-me-up, try the chai porridge or order a colourful acai bowl.

JURFOOD

Map 6; Øresundsvej 150D, Amager East; ///triads.channel.singled; jurfood.dk

Given its location right by the beach and far from the bustle of the city centre, Jurfood has a laidback vibe. On warm days, it's the haunt of beachgoers on their way to or from the nearby Amager

Amager Strand's great for a pre-brunch dip. Better yet, rent a stand-up paddleboard and skim across the sea.

Strand, roller skaters racing over for a coffee top-up and solo brunchers lazily sipping juice and watching the world go by from the window stools.

WULFF & KONSTALI

Map 6; Waterfront, Philip Heymans Allé 17–23, Hellerup; ///wink.roadmap.dissolve; www.wogk.dk

Shopping centre location? Check. Industrial interior? You got it. On the surface, Wulff & Konstali looks like any other pit-stop coffee shop, but the colourful and perfectly presented dishes here are made for long and lengthy brunches. Think banana and coconut granola topped with purple acai berries, and poppy-seed waffles with lime cream, apple crunch and a white chocolate sauce.

MAD & KAFFE

Map 2; Sønder Boulevard 68, Vesterbro; ///manages.lectures.stored; www.madogkaffe.dk

Mad & Kaffe is one of The Boulevard's staples, where the ravers of yesteryear – now driving pushchairs – rub shoulders with Vesterbro's current crop of creatives. They're all here to catch up – or reminisce – over a tapas-style brunch of small plates. Choose to order either three, five or seven items, depending on the size of your group and appetite.

» **Don't leave without** trying a poppy seed bun – yes, you can find them all over the city, but they won't taste as good as they do here.

Solo, Pair, Crowd

From quiet breakfasts on your own to raucous meetings with friends, brunch is always inclusive in Copenhagen.

FLYING SOLO

Take a seat

Atelier September is a favourite among creatives, who hunker down at their laptops here. If you're not one for a working brunch, bring your book or simply sit by the window and watch the world go by.

IN A PAIR

Brunch with a view

Sit back and soak up Amagertorv's bustling morning atmosphere at Café Norden. Pancakes, accompanied by a glass of champagne, are the ultimate date order.

FOR A CROWD

Start the party

Gather the gang for a long and lengthy brunch at Café Hoppes. Boozy beverages are always available and, on Fridays and Saturdays, DJs add to this restaurant's already lively atmosphere.

PALÆO

Map 6; Tuborg Havnevej 4–8, Hellerup; ///workshop.bucket.regime; www.palaeo.dk

PALÆO is where healthy folks go to recharge their batteries with super (and we mean super) food. Low-calorie filled wraps are the signature dish, the drinks menu is smoothie-heavy and even the burgers are piled high with cabbage, spinach and tomatoes.

» Don't leave without tickling your tongue with the sweet potato fries. Don't forgo the optional dip, which has just the right amount of tang.

CAFÉ LIVINGSTONE

Map 3; Sortedam Dossering 81, Østerbro; ///fruit.radio.tramps; www.livingstonecph.dk

Possibly the best alfresco brunch spot in the city, Café Livingstone occupies an enviable lakeside location. Soak up the sun and watch the runners zip by as you chow down on everything from chia-laden smoothie bowls to dripping merguez sausages.

MEYERS DELI

Map 2; Gammel Kongevej 107, Frederiksberg; ///tells.salad.escaping; www.meyers.dk

Ever wondered what your local mini mart would look like if it decided to open a gourmet café? Us neither, but here's your answer. Beside whirring refrigerators and shelves stacked with jars and tins, diners tuck into the likes of pancakes and burgers. If you're looking for a setting with more frills, book one of the mini glasshouses out back.

Bakeries

Denmark has long been known for its pastries, but Copenhagen's ambitious bakers have ripped up the old recipes and reimagined the lot, from crusty sourdough to the ubiquitous cardamom bun.

BAGERIET BRØD

Map 2; Enghave Plads 7, Vesterbro; ///penned.torn.removes; 20 70 04 22

Run by the creative folk behind grocery store-turned-hang-out spot Kihoskh, Brød (meaning bread) is cherished by local professionals, who flock here each morning to pick up loaves of its crisp, rustic bread before work. Later in the day, it's the haunt of Vesterbro mums, who can't resist their hungry kids' clamour for organic cinnamon snails.

JUNO THE BAKERY

Map 6; Århusgade 48, Østerbro; ///struts.bottled.regulate; info@junothebakery.com

With some of the city's finest carbs on offer, this corner bakery has people cycling to it from all over the city and willingly standing in line. The highlight? The cardamom buns, no question. Unlike the typically dense and heavy offerings, the *kardemummabulla* here are light, fluffy, buttery and always straight out of the oven. Delicious.

ANDERSEN BAKERY

Map 5; Thorshavnsgade 26, Islands Brygge; ///airtime.curo.icicles; www.andersen-bakery-eu.dk

When Shunsuke Takaki first tasted *wienerbrød* (Danish pastries) in 1959, he fell in love and started making them at his bakery in Japan. In 2008, he opened his own Copenhagen outpost and the city soon returned his affections, with locals journeying here even in the iciest months for a *fastelavnsbolle* (puff pastry with cream and jam).

» Don't leave without walking down to Havneparken *(p171)* to enjoy your sweet treats with a waterfront view – it's the perfect people-watching spot.

BAGERDYGTIGT

Map 6; Borgbjergsvej 39, Sydhavnen; ///gateway.crisps.bedding; www.bagerdygtigt.dk

This all-organic bakery is committed to producing zero waste, and whatever is left over at the end of the day is given to a local homeless shelter. Add the hearty rye sandwiches and inexpensive – by this city's standards – coffee and it's easy to see why Bagerdygtigt is so popular.

Try it!
BAKE UP A STORM

Learn how to make cinnamon rolls, traditional Danish rye bread and Claus Meyer's famous Øland wheat bread at his bakery in Nørrebro *(www.meyers.dk)*. The workshops last five hours.

MIRABELLE

Map 3; Guldbergsgade 29, Nørrebro;

///solar.guitars.artist; www.mirabelle-bakery.dk

Mirabelle is known for three things: almond croissants, sourdough bread and its owner, Christian Puglisi. This Noma alum has successfully married Italian craftsmanship with farm-to-table Danish produce, and seduced local hearts in the process.

HART BAGERI

Map 2; Gammel Kongevej 109B, Frederiksberg;

///resemble.emphasis.chose; www.hartbageri.com

Every weekend morning, chic Frederiksbergers line up outside this much-lauded bakery for top-notch, and super sustainable, baked goods. They're the work of Richard Hart – the former head baker of San Francisco's Tartine Bakery – and never fail to live up to the hype.

» Don't leave without trying the Cisco sourdough, which is delightfully crunchy on the outside, with an open crumb and slightly sour flavour.

LILLE BAKERY

Map 4; Refshalevej 213A, Refshaleøen;

///drama.farmed.dressy; www.lillegrocery.com

Situated in industrial Refshaleøen, lille is a quirky player on Copenhagen's artisan bakery scene. It's young and fun – don't be surprised if you catch the staff dancing to the music and sharing an inside joke. As for the menu, it really depends on what's in season, but you can always count on the *berliners* (doughnuts) and cinnamon rolls.

Liked by the locals

"Copenhagen has for a long time, in my opinion, had an incredible food scene. It's a pleasure to see its bakery scene becoming just as great. Having been to many places around the world myself, I definitely see Copenhagen at the very top in terms of quality."

JESPER GØTZ, CO-FOUNDER OF LILLE BAKERY

Smørrebrød Spots

Danes have been making smørrebrød (rye bread loaded with toppings) for centuries, and it's a classic that's still trending. At lunchtime, everyone from office workers to retired friends gather over these open sandwiches.

MØNTERGADE

Map 1; Gammel Mønt 41, Indre By; ///rebounds.fitter.lofts; www.montergade.dk

Never had smørrebrød before? Head to this stalwart of Danish cuisine for an introduction to Copenhagen's favourite lunch dish. The sharp staff here are on hand to help you navigate the classic toppings (such as herring or roast beef) and, if you're feeling a bit adventurous, they're always ready to bring out more curious options. Why not try the lobster tartare or fried camembert toppings?

CAFE DYREHAVEN

Map 2; Sønder Boulevard 72, Vesterbro; ///follow.salad.survive; www.dyrehavenkbh.dk

Located on Vesterbro's hippest street, in what was once a pub – spot the small wooden bar and mounted antlers – Café Dyrehaven has given the smørrebrød the millennial treatment. Here, the open-face sandwich has become a brunch item, with eggs Benedict, eggs vegetarian and – what else? – avocado toppings delighting the crowds of 20-somethings that flock here for weekend catch-ups.

RESTAURANT SCHØNNEMANN

Map 1; Hauser Plads 16, Indre By; ///glue.ensemble.refuse; www.restaurantschonnemann.dk

This local favourite has been a hub for informal business lunches since 1877. Settle in among the suits and you'll be treated to an array of authentic smørrebrød servings – plus a few seasonal specials. Be sure to wash them down with a potent shot of schnapps after, just like the rather laidback workers do.

» Don't leave without trying aquavit – a Scandi spirit distilled from grain and potatoes, and flavoured with herbs. There are more than 140 varieties on the menu at Restaurant Schønnemann.

SANS SOUCI

Map 2; Madvigs Allé 15, Frederiksberg; ///pram.animal.panthers; www.sanssouci.dk

A veritable classic, Sans Souci has been welcoming well-dressed diners and daters since it began in 1902. It may come as no surprise, given the restaurant's not-so-Scandi name, that the evening menu features classic French dishes. But at lunchtime this is *the* place to experience quintessential and quality smørrebrød – expect tasty toppings such as smoked salmon, picked herring and roast pork. For veggies? The potato toppings are irresistible.

Solo, Pair, Crowd

Whether you're grabbing lunch on the go or looking for a sit-down meal, there's a smørrebrød spot for you.

FLYING SOLO

Lunch by the lakes

Pick up some smørrebrød to go from Hallernes Smørrebrød at Torvehallerne market (Copenhagen's fave foodie hang-out). It's just round the corner from Ørsteds Park, which makes for a lovely picnic spot.

IN A PAIR

Smørrebrød with a view

Meyers i Tårnet is the perfect place for a sky-high romantic date or a catch-up with an old friend. Take in the breathtaking city views from Christiansborg Slot's tower while enjoying some New Nordic toppings.

FOR A CROWD

Tables for days

Peder Oxe's long tables can sit up to 25 smørrebrød-eaters. Need more space? A private room, overlooking Helligåndskirken (the Church of the Holy Spirit), hosts up to 70 guests.

KLINT

Map 4; Bredgade 68, Indre By; ///typical.together.film; www.designmuseum.dk

Once the refuel spots of sightseers, Copenhagen's museum cafés have earned a cult local following in recent years. One of the best? The Design Museum's Klint, now a go-to lunch stop for those who work in the showrooms nearby. Here, they devour smørrebrød under designer Kaare Klint's Frugtlygten (lamps that look like hanging fruit).

» Don't leave without taking an afternoon wander around the Design Museum's galleries.

AAMANNS DELI & TAKEAWAY

Map 3; Øster Farigmagsgade 10, København Ø; ///tourist.creeps.vipers; www.aamanns.dk

From the airy, plant-filled interior to the reimagined smørrebrød toppings, Aamanns feels like the cool new player on the scene. Try one of the three richly flavoured veggie options, topped with creamy mushrooms, tomatoes or potato chips – you won't regret it.

CAFE GAMMELTORV

Map 1; Gammeltorv 20, Indre By; letter.airless.rungs; www.cafegammeltorv.dk

With its gingham tablecloths and kitsch dishes, this grand old dame of traditional restaurants may look like it hasn't changed much over the past century, but don't let that fool you – it has vegan menus, after all. Smørrebrød are served *højtbelagt* (piled high) here, so come hungry.

Cheap Eats

Copenhagen may be a fairly expensive city, but locals know where to get bang for their buck. And when it comes to food, you don't need to pay Noma prices to enjoy something equally delicious.

DISTRICT TONKIN

Map 4; Store Kongensgade 71, Indre By; ///youth.darker.mammal; www.district-tonkin.com

Wander into this dimly lit nook and you'll immediately feel a world away. It all looks, smells and feels more like downtown Hanoi than central Copenhagen, with Vietnamese street food classics, such as banh mi (a crusty baguette filled with meat and veggies), on the menu – plus tofu versions for veggies. Be prepared – this place is heavy on the spice.

FOLKEHUSET ABSALON

Map 2; Sønder Boulevard 83, Vesterbro; ///fats.altering.slings; www.absaloncph.dk

What was once a stately church is now home to Copenhagen's cheapest daily buffet. Break bread with chatty students, pensioner patrons and families with young kids around long, multicoloured tables, where communal spirit reigns supreme. Beyond the kitchen's scrumptious offerings, Absalon also hosts daily events, including baby yoga, dance classes, bingo evenings and more.

» Don't leave without joining your new-found friends in a game of *rundt om bordet* (ping pong played around a circular table).

HOOKED

Map 2; Thorvald Bindesbølls Plads 36, Carlsberg Byen; ///checked.port.contexts; www.gethooked.dk

Foodies might rave about the Meatpacking District, but follow the adventurous types a little further out to family-friendly Carlsberg Byen – ducking under the famous Elefanttårnet on the way – and you'll discover plenty of excellent eateries, including this classic fish 'n' chips joint. Looking for something a bit more fancy? Opt for the lobster rolls or picture-perfect Poké bowls. Seafood always tastes best in the open air, so gobble up your grub in the quiet square out front.

BLUE HOUSE SANDWICH

Map 5; Torvegade 34C, Christianshavn; ///thrones.issue.lipstick; www.bluehouse.dk

Come lunchtime, you'll find everyone and anyone – from chilled-out Christiana folk to suited-and-booted businessmen – standing in line outside this basement sandwich shop. They come here to grab an immaculately rolled, and wallet-friendly, tuna salad or mozzarella and avocado sandwich. There's no indoor seating, so nab a spot on the cobbled, canalside street around the corner.

DEPANNEUR

Map 3; Rantzausgade 36, Nørrebro; ///shining.defends.lakes; www.depanneur.dk

Inspired by Montreal's *depanneurs* (convenience stores), this grocery shop-cum-restaurant is a pretty unique player on Copenhagen's foodie scene. After catching-up with a friend over draft beers and mouthwatering bagels (the ricotta and blackcurrant-filled one is our favourite), you can pick up a few essentials. How convenient is that?

HANZŌ

Map 2; Værnedamsvej 14, Vesterbro; ///kind.urban.moguls; www. madklubben.dk

Everything is influenced by east and southeast Asian street kitchens at Hanzō. First, there's the border-busting menu, with choices ranging from airy Chinese bao to hearty Japanese ramen, fresh Vietnamese summer rolls to tangy Korean BBQ. Then there's the interior itself. The main room is suitably colourful, yet moody, and there are even "back alley" tables, accessed through the kitchen.

DØP

Map 1; Købmagergade 52, Indre By; ///staging.berated.roof; www.xn--dp-lka.dk

Locals will say you haven't really experienced Copenhagen till you've tried a classic Danish hotdog, and DØP's two outposts serve up the best (you'll find the other branch by Helligåndskirken). Despite the old-fashioned stand, the food here's had a modern

This DØP stand is perfectly positioned to grab a dog before getting in the long line for Rundetårn.

makeover: the hotdogs are all organic and they're available in veggie versions too. Fast food done right if you ask us (and all the city's workers who pop by for lunch).

SASAA

Map 3; Blågårdsgade 2A, Nørrebro; ///silk.slate.clearly; www.sasaa.dk

Sasaa is Denmark's first Pan-African restaurant, representing cooking from across the continent. On the menu, which identifies the origin of each dish, you'll find everything from Somalian *suqaar* (fried beef and potatoes, served with a homemade chapati) to Senegalese peanut stew. But this isn't just a restaurant – Sasaa also hosts art, music and poetry events that explore the cultural diversity of this vast continent.

» Don't leave without ordering a hearty portion of jollof rice – a West African dish made up of long-grain rice, chicken, veggies and just the right amount of spice.

AMAGER KEBAB 2001

Map 5; Amagerbrogade 24, Amager; ///unroll.lovely.large; 32 95 00 16

If it were left to the modest sign alone, you could easily stroll straight past Amager Kebab 2001. Fortunately, the loud crowd of devoted locals that flock to this spot each evening make it difficult to miss. Here, they fill up on *durum* (flatbreads stuffed with hummus or succulent doner kebab) before hitting Copenhagen's bars and clubs. It has a really joyous vibe and even the staff look like they're having a party of their own behind the till.

Global Grub

You'd be missing out if you just stuck to New Nordic. Warm up with a comforting bowl of ramen, celebrate over Michelin-starred Mexican tacos – Copenhagen's culinary scene has a lot more to offer than you think.

GORDA

Map 2; Enghavevej 5, Vesterbro; ///incurs.atomic.richly; www.gorda.dk

A tiny enclave hidden on the unremarkable end of Enghavevej, Gorda is frequented by Vesterbro foodies who delight in having found this under-the-radar Argentinian joint. Street food is the order of the day here – expect ceviche, empanadas and veggie arepas.

REFFEN – COPENHAGEN STREET FOOD

Map 4; Refshalevej 167, Unit A, Refshaleøen; ///mental.coiling.until; www.reffen.dk

Can't decide what to eat tonight? Make for this organic street food mecca in grungy, but super-hip, Refshaleøen, which has 50-something alfresco stalls, each specializing in a different cuisine. As well as the city's largest selection of global grub, Reffen also offers Copenhagen's young guns a busy summer events calendar, with workshops, live

Hands down, the Real Greek stand serves the best gyros (kebabs), pita bread and tzatziki in the city.

music and games. No wonder it's so popular with groups of friends, who gather here to celebrate birthdays, promotions and the end of the working week.

BROENS GADEKØKKEN

Map 5; Strandgade 95, Indre By; ///exacted.animate.fault; www.broensgadekoekken.dk

If the idea of trekking to Reffen doesn't appeal, make for this summertime international food market near Nyhavn. It might be smaller than its more famous cousin, but Broens still presents an array of foodie treats to choose from. We recommend an all-American cheeseburger – served in an organic bun made with mashed potatoes – from Gasoline Grill or one of Indian street food specialist Dhubu's veggie curries, washed down with a pint of beer while watching the sunset.

SLURP RAMEN JOINT

Map 3; Nansensgade 90, Indre By; ///husbands.unites.hears; www.slurpramen.dk

Danes love slow, protracted dinners so how come a dish designed to be consumed at a rapid pace has proved so popular? With silky noodles and heartwarming broths, Slurp's offerings are simply delicious; when ramen is this good, why would you want to rush?

» **Don't leave without** ordering no 4 – a miso-based bowl, topped with pork belly, egg, bean sprouts, chilli cress, sesame seeds and chilli oil.

BÆST

Map 3; Guldbergsgade 29, Nørrebro; ///stencil.diet.beams; www.baest.dk

This organic Italian restaurant sources the majority of its ingredients from owner Puglisi's farm to the north of Copenhagen. You won't find fresher homemade burrata (made in the micro dairy above the restaurant) or more delicious wood-fired pizzas (topped with the likes of braised kale, nduja and pumpkin) anywhere else in the city.

TOMMI'S BURGER JOINT

Map 2; Høkerboderne 21–23, Kødbyen; ///sits.internal.fury; www.tommiburger.dk

This tiny Icelandic hang-out in the heart of the Meatpacking District has a very homely feel: from the hand-written cardboard menus nailed around the den to the smoky proximity of the kitchen to the counter. It's all very kid-friendly and, even on the coldest days, families wrapped in coats occupy the benches out front.

» **Don't leave without** ordering one of Tommi's unforgettable milkshakes. We love the super-sweet caramel shake.

HIJA DE SANCHEZ CANTINA

Map 6; Hamborg Plads 5, Nordhavn; ///occurs.binder.video; www.lovesanchez.com

Run by ex-Noma chef Rosio Sanchez, this cool cantina serves up the best Mexican street food in Copenhagen. Expect tasty dishes made with ingredients sourced from small, Mexican producers. Oh, and the decor? Pink and plant-filled – millennials and their mums love it.

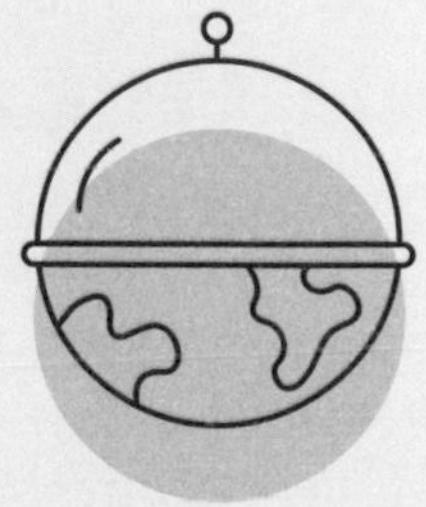

Liked by the locals

"A growing interest in global cuisine has in many ways redefined what it means to eat out in Copenhagen over the last few years, and the street food scene has grown immensely as a result."

MISCHA NIELSEN,
RESTAURANT MANAGER AND SOMMELIER

Special Occasion

Copenhageners are an understated bunch, but some occasions demand celebrations. Whether you're looking to toast an anniversary or want to make an event out of nothing, the city has a restaurant for you.

NO. 2

Map 5; Nicolai Eigtveds Gade 32, Christianshavn; ///magical.backers.flatten; www.nummer2.dk

Arresting harbour views, gleaming glassware and the occasional pop of a cork being sliced from a magnum of champagne by a sabre-wielding waiter: No. 2 might epitomize the fine-dining scene but its menu is packed with simple yet hearty crowd-pleasers that keep celebratory groups returning time after time. Think roasted turbot with Jerusalem artichokes and baked pumpkin with yoghurt.

MASH PENTHOUSE

Map 2; Arni Magnussons Gade 4, Kødbyen; ///device.choirs.infinite; www.mashsteak.dk

Fancy a top-notch steak dinner with epic city views? Head to this popular date night spot. At the Modern American Steak House (MASH) – located near the waterfront – graduate couples cosy up on plush seats to share bottles of full-bodied reds and tuck into gourmet beef. Those really looking to impress can splash out on Japanese Kobe, but there are also more reasonable Australian, Uruguayan, American and Danish cuts on the menu.

» Don't leave without digging your teeth into the Uruguayan sirloin steak – not as well known as Argentine cuts, but just as succulent.

GRO SPISERI

Map 6; Æbeløgade 4, Østerbro; ///harps.monopoly.shark; www.grospiseri.dk

Gro Spiseri floats high above the bustling streets below like a greenhouse in the sky. Oozing sustainability, community and cool, this farm-cum-restaurant is the unrivalled champion of Copenhagen's organic dining scene. There's no head chef in the kitchen and the greenhouse dining room has just one long table. The laidback crowd always gets chatting in no time – sharing stories about the farm and the afternoon cooking class, or exclaiming at the amazing sunset scenes.

Try it!
FARM YOUR FOOD

Lend a hand at Gro Spiseri's farm *(www.oestergro.dk)*. Volunteers spend an hour or two seeding, watering and harvesting before digging into a communal lunch. Keep an eye on the website for cooking classes, too.

LLAMA

Map 4; Lille Kongensgade 14, Indre By; ///loaders.fillers.worth; www.cofoco.dk

Basements tend to be dark and lifeless, but this subterranean restaurant is anything but. Maybe it's because of the handcrafted Mexican tiles adorning the walls and floors. Or perhaps it's the piquant Latin American menu, featuring classics like ceviche and *pimiento de padrón*. Loud, fun and youthful, this is a great place to hang out and celebrate life – no excuse necessary.

NOMA

Map 4; Refshalevej 96, Refshaleøen; ///tickles.roofer.airbag; www.noma.dk

We'd be mad not to feature this place, even if its reputation is down to its international fans rather than Copenhageners. If New Nordic cuisine is a religion, then this is its temple, where exceptional ingredients are paired in combinations that border on scientific

Yes, it's one of the best – and most expensive – restaurants in the world, but you don't have to pay Noma prices to sample its cooking. Run by the same people behind the world-famous restaurant, Popl is a little less fancy and a lot less pricey *(www.poplburger.com)*. The humble burger is the focus here, with patties made from organic Danish beef or quinoa tempeh, hand-produced in Noma's fermentation lab (yep, still swish).

experimentation. After years of saving and months of planning just to get a booking, those who dine here savour every moment of this once-in-a-lifetime opportunity. But, with no dress code and not a linen tablecloth in sight, it's surprisingly laidback once you're in.

ARK

Map 3; Nørre Farimagsgade 63, Indre By; ///altitude.loafer.glosses; www.restaurantark.dk

Thinking of turning vegan? This place will certainly persuade you. Since it opened in 2020, plant-based ARK has been making waves in the fine dining world, so trust us (and the critics) when we say the food here's top-notch. For the true ARK experience, try to resist peeking at the menu; rather, order the set seven courses blind and get ready for a thrilling journey through Copenhagen's finest gourmet-vegan cuisine.

RESTAURANT SILO

Map 6; Helsinki Gade, 17 Etage, Nordhavn; ///origin.decide.stoops; www.restaurantsilo.com

Made up of Tetris-like blocks, The Silo – an old grain store – is perhaps Nordhavn's most iconic building. And although the view of this brutalist structure from the ground is picture-perfect, the panorama offered from the restaurant on its 17th floor is worth a celebration all of its own. Add a fairly affordable menu and this is the perfect venue to toast even the most insignificant life event.

» Don't leave without trying the four-course Silo Menu. The dishes change daily, but you'll usually find servings of scallops and ribeye steak.

1

Sip and sift at
SORT KAFFE & VINYL

Not fully awake yet? Fuel up with a latte and pastry at record store-café-hybrid Sort, before rummaging through the eclectic vinyl collection.

2

Peruse the shelves of
THAI SUPERMARKET

Looking to cook up a Thai-style feast this weekend? Stock up on dragon fruit, durian, noodles and other scrumptious staples at this small but mighty supermarket.

3

Get artistic at
ANKER CHOKOLADE

Copenhageners take their sweet tooth seriously. Do the same and try your hand at a chocolate-making class, where you'll learn how to make Anker's famed *flødeboller* (chocolate-covered marshmallows).

The **Vodka Museum** *is home to the world's largest collection of vodka, housing over 1,600 bottles of the spirit.*

A 19th-century cattle market, ***Øksnehallen*** *is now a cultural space, hosting edgy exhibitions, fashion shows and flea markets.*

TORVET

KØDBYEN

RSKE-
RVET

Tuck in at KØDBYENS FISKEBAR

This meat hall-turned-fish restaurant is just the place to savour a seafood feast. If the sun's shining, nab a seat outside for an alfresco pre-dinner drink.

An afternoon dining in Kødbyen

Copenhagen's Meatpacking District, Kødbyen has been home to the city's thriving meat industry since the 19th century. With butchery becoming more efficient, the area has steadily evolved into a go-to foodie hotspot. What were once cattle markets and refrigerated warehouses are now cooler-than-cool restaurants and bars, serving up everything from fancy New Nordic tasting menus to no-frills BBQ fare. Ask any local where to go to get a taste of the city's diverse food scene and they'll answer Kødbyen.

1. Sort Kaffe & Vinyl
Skydebanegade 4, Kødbyen;
61 70 33 49
///outsiders.once.pushy

2. Thai Supermarket
Istedgade 134, Kødbyen;
www.thaisupermarket.dk
///bicker.launched.kilts

3. Anker Chokolade
Godsbanegade 17, Kødbyen;
www.ankerchokolade.dk
///printers.trails.careless

4. Kødbyens Fiskebar
Flæsketorvet 100, Kødbyen;
www.fiskebaren.dk
///outbid.action.classic

Øksnehallen *///snipped.husbands.boater*

Vodka Museum *///vows.supplier.massing*

DRINK

Cafés and bars are central to the city's social scene. Winter weekends pass catching up in cosy coffee shops, and summer nights are spent at lively alfresco bars.

Coffee Shops

Copenhagen's coffee scene is thriving, with local roasters and artisan cafés found in every corner of the city. In true Copenhagen style, blends tend to be brewed with sustainably and ethically sourced beans.

PROLOG COFFEE BAR

Map 2; Høkerboderne 16, Kødbyen; ///exacts.fend.toffee; www.prologcoffee.com

Run by a small team of award-winning coffee nerds and sustainability champions, Prolog takes coffee roasting and brewing seriously. The beans are responsibly sourced, the milk is delivered in reusable glass bottles and coffee grounds are composted at the end of the day.

PROPS COFFEE SHOP

Map 3; Blågårdsgade 5, Nørrebro; ///passion.panic.best; www.propscoffeeshop.dk

At this unpretentious Nørrebro coffee shop, cups of joe soon turn into bottles of beer and before you know it you're on a night out in Copenhagen's most lively neighbourhood. The best time to visit? In the summer months, when Props' lively pavement terrace is the starting point of the nightly Blågårdsgade café- and bar-hop.

ANDERSEN & MAILLARD

Map 3; Nørrebrogade 62, Nørrebro; ///fortunes.slippery.passions; www.andersenmaillard.dk

Coffee and baked goods: they just go together. Andersen & Maillard is a roastery, bakery and café in one, so the coffee and pastries are hot off the press and straight out of the oven. Located in an old bank, it attracts a solid crowd of Nørrebroders who appreciate impeccable interiors as much as their caffeine.

» **Don't leave without** indulging in an espresso soft serve, made from leftover milk and served on half a glazed croissant.

SONNY

Map 1; Rådhusstræde 5, Indre By; ///mindset.mixer.pokers; www.sonnycph.dk

Sonny is one of those places that people go to see and be seen. With its clean, monochrome interior and gingham-cushion-clad outdoor benches, this spot serves as a photo op for creatives and bloggers alike. Here, they clutch cups of coffee, brewed with beans from Aarhus-based roastery La Cabra.

Try it!
BECOME A BARISTA

The Coffee Collective, a sustainable coffee empire, runs courses to help you kick-start your barista career or simply master the art of brewing an aromatic cup of black gold at home *(www.coffeecollective.dk)*.

CAFÉ DET VIDE HUS

Map 3; Gothersgade 113, Indre By; ///sitting.enable.wakes; 60 61 20 02

The main reason to pop into this thoroughly unpretentious coffee joint is to say "hej" to the owner, who is invariably found at the helm of the coffee machine. Claus Dalsgaards knows just about everyone worth knowing on the city's speciality coffee scene, from local micro roasters to international legends. Oh, and he makes a mean brew.

FOVL

Map 6; Sneppevej 2, Nordvest; ///purely.seasons.froth; www.fovl.dk

Few visitors venture out to Nordvest, but this young, hip and culturally diverse neighbourhood has a lot to offer, including Fovl. With its casual interior and welcoming crowd, this cosy coffee joint will make you feel instantly at home. So, pull up a seat and soak up the *hyggelig* vibes.

DEMOCRATIC COFFEE

Map 1; Krystalgade 15, Indre By; ///logic.likes.freezing; 40 19 62 37

Coffee and books – it's a marriage made in heaven. Located inside the public library, Democratic Coffee is buzzing with students and wannabe intellectuals, discussing literature and sipping swirling brews. The best reading spot is by the window, where you can occasionally look up from your book to watch the world go by.

» **Don't leave without** joining one of the library's many events. There are book clubs and meet-ups, as well as communal singing (a very Danish activity), which takes place every Wednesday at 8:30am.

Liked by the locals

"The speciality coffee scene in Copenhagen is driven by many small, innovative actors, each bringing their own approach to the table, but generally sharing a passion for lighter roasts and aromatic blends."

KLAUS THOMSEN, FOUNDER OF THE COFFEE COLLECTIVE

Alfresco Tipples

Copenhagen's long summer evenings are made for outdoor drinking. During the warmer months, locals flock to open-air venues to sip fruity cocktails, sharp wines and refreshing beers until the sun finally sets.

GREEN ISLAND OF COPENHAGEN

Map 5; Kalvebod Brygge 9, Vesterbro; ///aged.speak.offshore; www.green-island.dk

At lunchtime, this little floating bar throngs with Vesterbro's financiers, but come the evening these city slickers are outnumbered by carefree 20-somethings, who loaf about on the beanbags. Join them over Aperol spritzes and cold beers, while taking in the watery views.

DEN VANDRETTE WINEBAR

Map 4; Havnegade 53A, Indre By; ///flames.diamond.breezy; www.denvandrette.dk

You might be smack bang in Nyhavn (ie tourist central) but sit down at this pavement café and you'll feel like you've been transported to a sleepy seaside town. Maybe it's the harbour view, the gentle, salty breeze or the fact that chilled glasses of wine are often accompanied by plates of tasty tapas.

LA BANCHINA

Map 4; Refshalevej 141, Refshaleøen; ///sparks.frowns.canyons; www.labanchina.dk

This restaurant-bar isn't just a summertime spot: people come to swim off La Banchina's jetty all year round. The sweating summer crowd cools down with a dip and icy drinks, while brave winter bathers recover from their ice baths with steaming cups of coffee.

» **Don't leave without** warming up in the on-site sauna after your bracing laps in the winter waters.

ILLUM ROOFTOP

Map 1; Købmagergade 20, Indre By; ///strides.flying.bossy; www.illum.dk

Who would have thought that a shopping mall could claim the city's best views? Overlooking bustling Amagertorv, the terrace off ILLUM's food hall is a sun-drenched oasis, popular with mothers seeking a moment of calm, and – come 5pm – the after-work crowd.

What could possibly be more under the radar than having a drink on a retired ferry? *Ellen*, or Kontiki Bar as it's now known, spends its pensioned days spoiling younger generations with some of the best alfresco parties in Copenhagen. Anything can happen here. You could be invited along to a private party in the captain's bar upstairs or to take a late-night skinny dip *(www.kontikibar.dk)*.

Solo, Pair, Crowd

Whatever the size of your party, Copenhagen has an alfresco bar or café for you.

FLYING SOLO

Drink by design

Soak up the waterfront views from the DAC café, above the Danish Architecture Centre. With a cheeky glass of wine in hand, you can muse over whether the Blox building below is an eyesore or an absolute masterpiece.

IN A PAIR

Shed for two

Romance may not be the first thing that comes to mind when you think of a wooden hut attached to a church, but Café Riga's peaceful location and affordable drinks make it one of the city's best date spots.

FOR A CROWD

Hit the roof

Whether savouring tea and cake, tucking into a charcuterie board or catching up over a signature aperitivo, your gang will love Tramonto Rooftop's terrace.

LUFTKASTELLET

Map 4; Ofelia Plads, Indre By; ///thrilled.organic.guitar; www.luftkastellet.dk

Luftkastellet has a very community-centric vibe. Sitting on Ofelia Plads – the jetty-cum-square – this is where people come to salute the sun, dance up a sweat and cheer on Denmark in World Cup matches. If that all sounds far too energetic, soak up the harbour views with a frosty cocktail in hand.

HALVANDET

Map 4; Refshalevej 325, Refshaleøen; ///toolkit.tapes.explorer; www.halvandet.dk

It may be located on the very edge of grungy Refshaleøen, but this beach bar feels distinctly Caribbean (though perhaps minus a few degrees). Here, sun-worshippers relax on plush, white loungers or perch at the umbrella-shaded bar while swaying to the nightly DJ sets.

KAYAK BAR

Map 5; Børskaj 12, Indre By; ///outbid.rocker.arching; www.kayakbar.dk

Just one after-work drink always escalates into a wild night at Kayak. This floating wooden jetty is packed with an ever-changing crowd, thanks to its constant water-based traffic. Every so often, a boat will rock up, delivering some of its party to the bar and gaining some new revellers before rowing off again. It all makes for a super fun night.

» **Don't leave without** renting a kayak – it's in the name after all. You're bound to get splashed, but exploring the canals is more than worth it.

Wine Bars

Pick the brains of the city's passionate sommeliers and mingle with fellow oenophiles in these cosy, hygge-fuelled bars – you might even discover a new penchant for natural wine or Danish varieties.

TERROIRISTEN

Map 3; Jægersborggade 52, Nørrebro; ///pens.pricing.replace; www.terroiristen.dk

You'll find this modest but very important player on the city's natural wine scene deep underground. Terroiristen is a basement bar-meets-bottle shop run by Stefan Jensen, who's always on hand to offer recommendations and answer any questions about the differences between organic and biodynamic grapes.

» **Don't leave without** ordering an Eastern European variety with Stefan's help. You never know, it might become your new go-to order.

MELÔ

Map 1; Peder Hvitfeldts Stræde 17, Indre By; ///sailed.help.soils; 23 81 64 59

Tucked off Kultorvet, this cosy spot feels just like your best friend's living room, complete with funky vases and cool prints. Run by a brother-and-sister team, the vibe is informal and the atmosphere's

Melô runs regular tasting events. Check its Facebook page for upcoming port or cider evenings.

endlessly welcoming. Draw up a seat and be prepared to get stuck into board games or bingo with a group of strangers that'll quickly become friends.

VINBAREN VESTERBRO TORV

Map 2; Svendsgade 1, Vesterbro; ///toxic.until.headache; www.vinveto.dk

In classic cooler-than-cool Vesterbro style, this wine bar is rustic and unpretentious. The wooden floor is a bit wonky, the lamps don't match and its ever-changing menu is penned on a whiteboard for an old-school touch. But don't be fooled into thinking that the selection isn't ambitious – the sommelier-educated staff know their grape juice repertoire and won't hesitate to share their know-how with you as they pour out your glass.

VED STRANDEN 10

Map 1; Ved Stranden 10, Indre By; ///bunk.almost.tonight; www.vedstranden10.dk

Stepping inside this unique wine bar might feel like entering a private home, albeit one that's featured in a glossy interior design magazine. The space is divided into intimate rooms, decorated with house plants, coffee-table books and one-of-a-kind objects. Where better for a cosy date night or friendly tapas session? If you're looking for a more raucous evening with a bunch of mates, don't discount this place either. On summer evenings, its sun-drenched, canalside terrace becomes one of the hottest alfresco party spots in town.

VORES VINBAR

Map 2; Sønderboulevard 105, Vesterbro; ///insist.showed.reunion; www.voresvinbar.dk

A small bar focused on Danish wines and owned by a cooperative of ten friends, Vores Vinbar's communal approach to business is reflected in the friendly exchanges you're likely to have over the counter. Add its unassuming interior, mood lighting and comforting tapas, and this bar represents – dare we say it – hygge at its finest.

TAPS WINEBAR CPH

Map 4; Store Regnegade 26A, Indre By; ///daily.enlarge.chills; www.tapswinebar.dk

With a group of friends that can never agree on which bottle to order? Enter TAPS. A fresh and innovative concept on Copenhagen's wine scene, this self-service wine bar has a

Wine doesn't exactly come cheap in Copenhagen, but there are some affordable spots if you know where to look. Tucked away in the Kastellet complex, Løgismose Vin, Mad og Delikatesser is a delicatessen-meets-bottle shop-meets-wine bar that sells vintages at shelf price *(www.loegismose.dk)*. It's such great value that the city's sommeliers flock here on their days off to check out the latest varieties and replenish their personal wine stores.

massive and varied selection of vintages on tap, ranging in price, origin and taste profiles. On arrival, you're equipped with a preloaded "wine card", which fills half or brimming glasses at the touch of a button. A word of warning: pace yourself if you plan on avoiding a sore head in the morning.

POMPETTE

Map 3; Møllegade 3, Nørrebro; ///altitude.stormed.elastic; www.pompette.dk

Where can you find the most reasonably priced natural wine in Copenhagen? At this small bar, nestled down a quiet side street off bustling Nørrebrogade, where all glasses are 50DKK. Couple its affordable wine with generous charcuterie and cheeseboards and it's no wonder Pompette's street-side tables are always occupied.

NÆRVÆR

Map 5; Strandgade 87, Indre By; ///kennels.gained.lighter; www.naervaer.dk

With its high ceilings and cavernous size, this central wine bar could have felt soulless. Fortunately, its owners (and renowned Danish designers Norm Architects) know the value of low lighting and a clever layout, and the result is a classy space, filled with cosy corners. It's the perfect place to take a date who loves design as much as wine.

» **Don't leave without** hopping into the water for a pre-drink swim – the wine bar overlooks a sheltered part of the harbour.

Cocktail Joints

Copenhagen's cocktail bars mix up innovative concoctions that are no less inventive (or resourceful) than the dishes dreamed up in New Nordic kitchens. Get ready to tickle your taste buds.

JOJO VESTERBRO

Map 2; Sundevedsgade 4, Vesterbro; ///animate.back.enable; www.jojovesterbro.dk

Combining the stylish interior and drinks menu of a cocktail bar with the friendly, faithful crowd of a brown bar, Jojo Vesterbro is always a popular post-work choice. And with drinks starting at only 50DKK a pop, you can see why. Join the regulars in the bright pink-and-blue interior over espresso martinis, palomas or low-alcohol options (made with organic ingredients, of course).

BRØNNUM

Map 4; August Bournonvilles Passage 1, Indre By; ///magic.healthier.launched; www.bronnumcph.dk

We thought twice about letting the secret out about Brønnum, but this place is too good to miss. On the surface, it may seem like any other bar in Copenhagen – or even the world. But once you move past the bright and light main bar and venture deeper into Brønnum's fleet of six rooms, everything becomes darker, more intimate and increasingly clandestine. It's the quintessential speakeasy.

» Don't leave without attending a 90-minute "Brønnum Session". You'll learn all about your favourite tipple – be it champagne, gin, bourbon, rum or, indeed, cocktails – and taste a few, too.

MÓSHÙ COCKTAIL CLUB

Map 4; Lille Kongensgade 8, Indre By; ///changing.chatted.pose

Inspired by Shanghai's intimate cocktail bars, Móshù emulates the Chinese city's moody vibe. Think giant red lanterns, beautifully painted porcelain pots and faded printed wallpaper. And the cocktails? These dry-ice-topped concoctions wouldn't be out of place in the Paris of the East either. It's all pretty luxe, much like its owner, former Danish *X Factor* judge and music producer Remee Jackman. Book a table via social media.

VANG & BAR

Map 2; Ingerslevsgade 200, Vesterbro; ///doctors.clashes.warping; www.vangandbar.com

Vang & Bar puts the easy in speakeasy. In a departure from the American cocktail tradition, everything about this joint is simple, understated and (most importantly) fairly priced. Opt for the "cocktail experience", a set menu of three drinks, all made from seasonal, organic ingredients. You could get an apricot pisco sour, raspberry negroni or coffee mint julep. Delicious!

Solo, Pair, Crowd

A quiet evening, a great first date, a fun night out: whatever you're looking for, a cocktail bar is the answer.

FLYING SOLO

Make a new friend

Strangers quickly become best friends at Blume. This hidden basement bar is where DJs come to hang out in their downtime, so you might even leave with an invite to one of the hottest clubs in town.

IN A PAIR

Vintage date

Duck and Cover has an irresistible 60s vibe, modelled on the home of the owner's grandmother. Think slouchy leather armchairs and plenty of house plants. As a result, it's cosy and romantic without being clichéd.

FOR A CROWD

The more the merrier

On the nightly Vesterbro-Nørrebro bar-hop? Make a stop at Bar Gensyn before pushing on to a club. Here, you can challenge the gang to a game of pool while sipping negronis.

BRASS MONKEY

Map 2; Enghavevej 31, Vesterbro; ///appeal.brushing.initial; www.brassmonkey.dk

Most of the folks crammed into this little cavern have likely got sidetracked on their way home from somewhere else – usually a house party or a meal with old mates. They're not really here for the cocktails, but for the chance to bust a move on the tiny dance floor, fuelled by an eclectic mix of reggae, calypso, rock and R'n'B.

LIDKOEB

Map 2; Vesterbrogade 72B, Vesterbro; ///accusing.feast.recently; www.lidkoeb.dk

Standing behind the old pharmacy counter, Lidkoeb's mixologists craft cocktails with as much skill and care as their forebears did medicines. Today's fortifying elixirs are made from the likes of teapot bitters, quince cordial and cashew orgeat. Sounds like just what the doctor ordered.

» **Don't leave without** sampling The Grapes of Wrath. A mix of plum cordial, Oloroso sherry and cognac, it puts the "o" in "old fashioned".

BALDERDASH

Map 1; Valkendorfsgade 11, Indre By; ///edicts.audibly.balance; www.balderdash.dk

At first glance, Balderdash looks like a classic American cocktail joint, with its curved wooden bar and low lighting. But this place has a typically Danish menu, with a focus on fresh, natural – and sometimes foraged – ingredients, such as deer heart, nettle and mushroom.

Breweries

Denmark has a long and rich brewing heritage, dominated by world-famous brands (hello, Carlsberg). But Copenhagen's microbrewers and big craft names, such as Mikkeller, are keeping the scene fresh.

BAGHAVEN

Map 4; Refshalevej 169B, Refshaleøen; ///afford.replaces.bouncing; www.mikkeller.com

If Mikkeller is a craft beer empire, then this is its crown jewel. This huge brewery produces sour, fermented beers using yeast and bacteria cultures created from foraged fruits in the on-site microbiology lab. How Copenhagen is that?

» **Don't leave without** trying one of Mikkeller's non-alcoholic beers. There are no-abv IPAs and gose-style beers, as well as fruity brews, on the menu.

KØLSTERS TOLV HANER

Map 3; Rantzausgade 56, Nørrebro; ///linked.swelling.coasted; 32 20 94 84

Everyone who comes here tells their friends (who tell their friends, and so on). So, it's little wonder that this place is always packed with 20-somethings and has that good-time vibe Nørrebro is all about.

It has a particularly festival-like feel in summertime, when colourful fairy lights illuminate its buzzing outdoor tables. And what about the beer? Expect light brews, served in small glasses – the perfect excuse to try several.

WARPIGS

Map 2; Flæsketorvet 25, Kødbyen; ///crisp.lows.probably; www.warpigs.dk

Mikkeller teamed up with American brewery 3 Floyds to create a stellar brewpub, and this is the result. In homage to classic Texan breweries, meat and beer are all you'll find on the menu here (okay, that's not strictly true: there's also organically sweetened, fair trade soda that puts Diet Coke to shame). The 22 taps deliver American-Danish style craft beer, brewed at the in-house brewery, and the food menu speaks to the spirit of the Meatpacking District (and this former slaughterhouse's past life). Think spare ribs, meat smoked overnight, pork shoulders and more.

Shh!

People Like Us *(www.peoplelikeus.dk)* is on a mission. Run by a charity that supports socially marginalized groups, this brewery aims to create jobs, challenge preconceptions and (you guessed it) brew great beer. It's well worth crossing the Stadsgraven canal to get to under-the-radar Amager where PLU hosts monthly workshops, which merge all manner of pastimes with a love of beer.

Liked by the locals

"As a home brewer, I'm always looking out for microbreweries that offer something a bit off the beaten track: a sour, a lambic, maybe an exceptionally juicy IPA. And Copenhagen's scene has all this and more."

JEANIFER BREAKLING, HOME BREWER AND SENIOR COPYWRITER AT KAYAK

MIKKELLER & FRIENDS

Map 3; Stefansgade 35, KLD, Nørrebro; ///composer.tests.popped; www.mikkeller.com

This cool off shoot of Mikkeller is a hub for local diehards, who seem to perch on the same wooden stools all day. And who can blame them when there's over 40 taps to try? As well as Mikkeller's brews, expect guest beers from local up-and-coming breweries.

» **Don't leave without** popping into the adjoining Koelschip bar, which specializes in lambic brews. If you've never heard of this Belgian beer, now's the time to try it.

TAPHOUSE

Map 1; Lavendelstræde 15, Indre By; ///spike.bricks.apricot; www.taphouse.dk

It's a craft beer haven in here, with 60-plus taps dripping a changing selection of brews. Every time a new beer is added to the menu, it flashes up on Taphouse's electronic board. Don't know your pale ales from your Pilsners? No bother, this board – and the friendly staff – will guide you through the taste profiles, origins and abv of each brew.

BRUS

Map 3; Guldbergsgade 29F, Nørrebro; ///migrate.exacts.swan; www.tapperietbrus.dk

The on-site brewery's the star of the show here. Brus's 13 fermentation tanks are constantly brewing new flavours for an army of Nørrebro's coolest. As well as the beers, they love this brewpub for its pop-up events, such as Portuguese fado nights and Korean food festivals.

Brush up on brewing history at
VISIT CARLSBERG

Take a tour of Carlsberg's old brewery and visitor centre to discover the history of the Danish brand (tastings are available).

Lunch at
TRAMONTO ROOFTOP

Atop a 19th-century building that once stored beer, this Italian restaurant offers amazing views of Carlsberg Byen.

Fill up at
RAMEN TO BÍIRU

Ready to dive into the craft beer scene? Enjoy a range of Mikkeller home brews and generous bowls of miso ramen at this pit stop.

Stretch your legs in the
J C JACOBSEN HAVE

This verdant slice of green was once the private garden of the Carlsberg family. It's now a public park loved by locals; keep an eye out for the unique hanging gardens.

Mikkeller's HQ *is just around the corner from Carlsberg's old haunt, but this brand's history is much more recent – it was founded in 2007.*

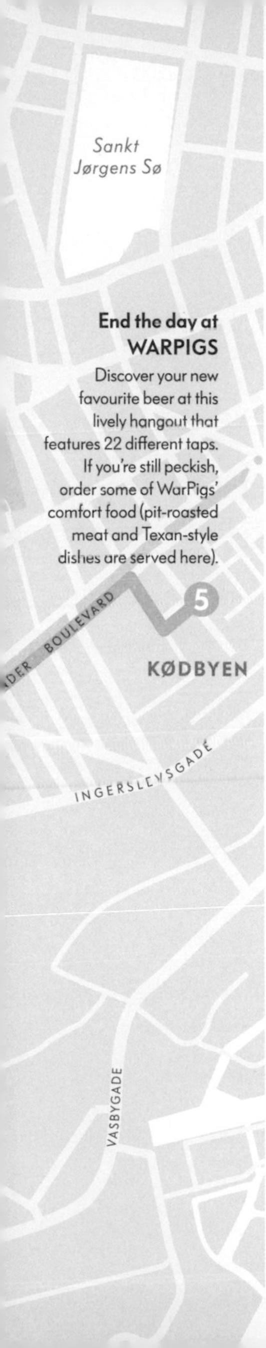

Sankt Jørgens Sø

End the day at WARPIGS

Discover your new favourite beer at this lively hangout that features 22 different taps. If you're still peckish, order some of WarPigs' comfort food (pit-roasted meat and Texan-style dishes are served here).

5

BOULEVARD

KØDBYEN

INGERSLEVSGADE

VASBYGADE

An afternoon of brewing history

Denmark's love of beer can be traced right back to the Vikings, who regularly knocked back the good stuff. Brewers' guilds started popping up in the 1500s but it wasn't until Carlsberg was founded in 1847 that Copenhagen became world famous for its brewing. These days, it's all about Mikkeller and the craft beer revolution. For a look (and taste) of the beer scene, head to Carlsberg Byen, an area once dominated by the famed brewery, before strolling to Vesterbro, home of modern beer-makers.

1. Tramonto Rooftop
Bryggernes Plads 7,
Carlsberg Byen;
www.tramonto.dk
///tinkle.sharper.clues

2. Visit Carlsberg
Gamle Carlsbergvej 11,
Carlsberg Byen;
www.visitcarlsberg.com
///packages.insist.breathed

3. J C Jacobsen Have
Olivia Hansens Gade 2,
Carlsberg Byen;
www.carlsbergfondet.dk
///proofs.winter.lifted

4. Ramen to Bíiru
Enghavevej 58, Vesterbro;
www.ramentobiiru.dk
///jacket.signal.plugged

5. WarPigs
Flæsketorvet 25, Kødbyen;
www.warpigs.dk
///crisp.lows.probably

Mikkeller's HQ
///fewest.sang.spit

SHOP

Danish design is legendary and the capital's indie and vintage stores won't disappoint those looking for cool, clean pieces. Bonus point: many stores are eco-friendly, too.

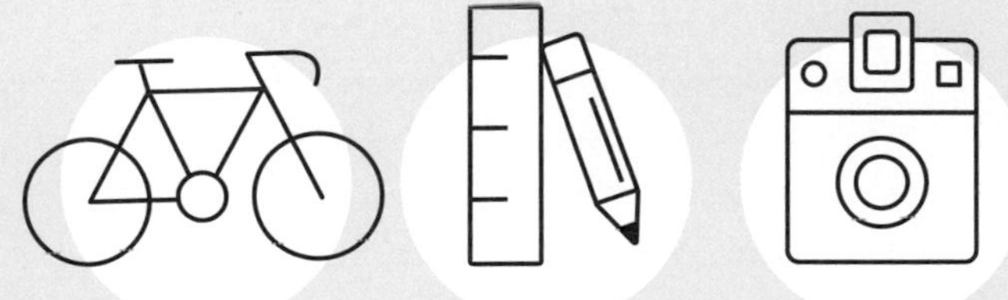

Vintage Gems

Eco-conscious Copenhageners have an insatiable hunger for all things sustainable, cyclical and reusable. Luckily for them, the city is brimming with second-hand flea markets and vintage boutiques.

I BLAME LULU

Map 3; Rosenvængets Allé 8, Østerbro; ///lift.circling.shuttle; www.iblamelulu.com

Been coveting a dress from cool Copenhagen brand Stine Goya? After those Stella McCartney shoes that all the influencers have from a few seasons ago? You can bet on finding them at I Blame Lulu. Expect immaculate rails and a generally more upmarket feel than most vintage shops, with fashionistas – who are themselves a source of style inspiration – eyeing each item expertly.

STUDENTERHUSET'S LOPPEMARKED

Map 1; Købmagergade 52, Latinerkvarteret; ///cones.goggles.hopping; www.studenterhuset.com

Hungover students doing the Sunday rounds after a big night out haunt this monthly flea market. In fact, they may well have enjoyed live music, beer and board games here the previous evening, before

"The Student House" did its monthly reinvention act. Join the masses and wander between the rows of cheap patterned shirts, explore the incredible collection of jazzy knitwear and try on some funky slogan T-shirts.

ANTIK K

Map 1; Knabrostræde 13, Indre By; ///imagined.label.unveils; www.antikk.dk

Despite its diminutive size, Antik K is brimming with everything from antique wooden toys to oil paintings. The crowded shelves, complete with the odd cobweb here and there, emit a dated vibe that complements the shop's age-old trinkets, but don't be fooled – there are treasures to be found here. Look out for Georg Jensen silverware and the distinct blue and white of Royal Copenhagen porcelain.

» **Don't leave without** bagging a classic Kay Bojesen or Tekno toy. They really don't make them like they used to.

TIMES UP VINTAGE

Map 1; Krystalgade 4, Latinerkvarteret; ///prompt.jaws.impaired; www.timesupshop.com

Don't be surprised if you run into a well-known fashion designer searching for inspiration for their next collection here. The rails of couture – think Versace bomber jackets, Moschino minidresses and YSL sequin suits – have been collected and curated from around the world by Times Up's globetrotting owner, Jesper Richardy. Sounds pricey? It is, but you can still find some bargains here if you hunt hard enough.

EDIE

Map 3; Østerbrogade 128, Østerbro; ///tugging.amuses.gazed; www.edie.dk

Reclaiming the phrase "so last season", Edie is stocked with last year's runway gems, now marked down to bargain prices. Expect pieces from cool local brands – we're talking floaty floral dresses from Stella Nova and MENU's minimalist, monochrome homeware *(p91)* – at 40 to 70 per cent cheaper than before.

VERAS MARKET

Map 6; Bispeengbuen, Nørrebro; ///posts.tidying.nasal; www.verasvintage.dk

When stylist Rebecca Vera Stahnke struggled to find an easy way to purge and replenish her wardrobe, she decided to do something about it – and the fashion conscious of Copenhagen are so happy that she did. A fun atmosphere prevails at this giant clothing swap party, where

We've got just the thing to light up your life. Hidden on the edge of Vesterbro, on an otherwise residential street, is Lurgan Vintage *(www.lurgan.dk)*, the best antique lighting shop in the city. Inside you'll find glass pendant lights, architectural standing lamps and other vintage fixtures. All eras and aesthetics are covered – from Art Deco to industrial chic – so you're bound to have a lightbulb moment (sorry) and find just the thing to complete your room.

local style mavens exchange, buy and sell their pre-loved pieces. A browse is always a pleasure, but those in the know stalk the website to find out about the next flash sale, when prices are slashed even lower.

» Don't leave without politely negotiating the price. Haggling isn't a thing in Copenhagen, but if you buy in bulk or bring the right vibes, you may end up with a steal.

PRAG

Map 2; Vesterbrogade 98A, Vesterbro; ///airless.readings.evenings; www.pragcopenhagen.com

Looking for an oh-so-perfect outfit to wear the next time you hit up Vesterbro's dance floors? Prag is the only shop you need to visit. Here, you'll find row upon row of sequin tops, pastel dresses and retro sportswear. And as it's open seven days a week (unlike Copenhagen's other vintage stores), it's there for those "emergencies" when you just don't have anything to wear.

KØBENHAVN K CHARITY SHOP

Map 1; Studiestræde 32, Latinerkvarteret; ///clocked.chucks.study; www.koebenhavnk.com

True vintage shoppers love the thrill of the search, and locating the entrance to this second-hand store is a taster for the quest to come. (Hint: look for the swinging "K" sign.) The hunt continues inside, with thrifty shoppers rifling through buckets of shoes and piles of Levis to find their new favourite threads. It's packed to the rafters with pieces, so go when you have the time to really root through the rails.

Danish Design

Understated furniture, minimal ceramics and sustainably crafted textiles: Copenhagen's design scene is world-class. Stop by one of these gems to take home an iconic piece of craftsmanship.

YONOBI

Map 1; Løvstræde 1, Indre By;
///blend.hampers.instead; www.itsyonobi.com

Owner Nanna Egebjerg prides herself on discovering independent artists from around the world. Everything here – including stone vases from Taiwan, elegant bowls made in Sweden and cute French ceramics – is handcrafted and handpicked. Swing by to find that one-of-a-kind present for your favourite person.

Try it!
TAKE TO THE WHEEL

Create your own mug or bowl at one of Yonobi's pottery classes. Choose from an evening, day or weekend wheel-throwing workshop, and learn from, surely, some of the loveliest potters out there.

DANSK MADEFORROOMS

Map 2; Istedgade 80, Vesterbro;

///join.cherub.puddles; www.danskshop.com

Showcasing a carefully curated collection of local furniture and homeware, this little store is the perfect intro to contemporary Danish design. The space itself is bright and minimal, letting the products speak for themselves. And what products they are: elegant lights, quirky vases and clean-cut furniture pieces.

ILLUMS BOLIGHUS

Map 1; Amagertorv 10, Indre By;

///slippery.spark.thanks; www.illumsbolighus.dk

Design-savvy Danes can't help but stop and stare at the dazzling window displays of this beloved store – a purveyor to the royal family no less. Most give in to temptation and end up losing an hour or two here, reappearing with some precious porcelain and glassware.

» **Don't leave without** popping down the street to ILLUM – an extravagant shopping mall with an enticing basement food hall.

VESTERGAARD MØBLER

Map 5; Torvegade 55–7, Christianshavn;

///twists.petted.vest; www.vester-moebler.dk

What was once a humble carpentry shop in Vesterbro is now an iconic Christianshavn design destination. Loyal locals, who value the store's 100 years of know-how, flock here each weekend to scour the timeless collection of Scandi furniture.

DESIGNER ZOO

Map 2; Vesterbrogade 137, Vesterbro; ///parkway.lucky.vibrate; www.designerzoo.dk

In addition to selling a vast and varied selection of ceramics, glassware and furniture, this quirky shop runs open workshops to provide insights into the craft of pottery, jewellery, woodwork and more. Bring a friend and hone your crafty skills here alongside moustachioed woodworkers and kooky ceramicists.

HAY HOUSE

Map 1; Østergade 61, Indre By; ///snappy.riot.monk; www.hay.dk

You'll find all the usual markers of stylish Scandi design in this emporium, but they've had a bit of a playful makeover. Follow young professionals and influencers into the store and you'll discover funky wall clocks, oddly shaped vases, spiral candles and pastel-coloured storage crates – perfect for giving your apartment a little lift.

» **Don't leave without** soaking up the view of Amagertorv – arguably Copenhagen's prettiest square – from the top floor.

STILLEBEN

Map 3; Frederiksborggade 22, Indre By; ///chipper.encoded.union; www.stilleben.dk

Designers looking for inspiration, anxious partners searching for the perfect anniversary present and 20-somethings hoping to quickly pick up a birthday gift for a friend: all of them know that Stilleben stocks the answer. In the unlikely scenario that you can't find exactly what you're looking for among the colourful selection – we particularly love the art prints – the friendly staff are ready with suggestions.

PAUSTIAN

Map 1; Niels Hemmingsens Gade 24, Indre By;
///oblige.liquids.delved; www.paustian.com

Beautiful furniture deserves to occupy an equally beautiful setting, and what's more elegant than an 18th-century bank complete with vaulted marble ceilings and Corinthian columns? Even Paustian's basement vaults have been transformed into unique showrooms, where interior design tastemakers and arty enthusiasts contemplate wares by both local and international brands. While the majority of Paustian's stock doesn't come cheap (though we'd argue it's always a good investment), the stationery, glassware and textiles are more affordable for those of us on a budget.

Shh!

Take a trip out to Nordhavn for a visit to The Audo *(www.theaudo.com)*. As an office for Danish furniture brand MENU, a high-end hotel, a café and a concept store, this hybrid space is a unique player on the design scene. Pop by the concept store for top-notch Danish designs, including new stock from MENU, as well as exclusive items from well-known and up-and-coming international creators.

Bike Shops

You probably know by now that Copenhageners love their bikes, with half of locals commuting on two wheels each day. Join the city-wide cycling community by checking out the bikes at one of these indie shops.

CHRISTIANIA CYKLER

Map 5; Fabriksområdet 91, Christiania; ///toward.wake.majority; www.christianiacykler.dk

The Christiania cargo bike is a staple on the cycling scene. Locals balance everything from shopping bags to furniture in the front box, and parents on the school run furiously pedal their trailer of gleeful children along cycle lanes. Come to this store to see where it all started way back in 1984, when blacksmith Lars Engstrøm crafted the first cargo bike as a birthday present for his girlfriend, Annie.

BIKE COPENHAGEN

Map 1; Nikolaj Plads 34, Indre By; ///pockets.enjoy.racks; www.bikecopenhagen.dk

Looking to cycle the Danish way? Look no further. Bike Copenhagen will set you up with the perfect set of wheels to blend in with the locals. Choose between the home-grown Christiania cargo bike and the

Finnish-designed JOPO – a cool and colourful bicycle that's quickly won Copenhageners over. Once you've picked your trusty steed, set off on a cycling adventure, carving your own route around the city or joining one of Bike Copenhagen's fun two-hour tours.

CAFÉ VÉLO

Map 3; Frederiksborggade 31, Indre By; ///quantity.courier.raking; www.cafevelocopenhagen.com

There's a real hipster hum to this bike shop-meets-café, with its vintage bikes propped up against the bare brick wall and the smell of fresh coffee filtering through the air. Wander over on a Sunday morning and you'll see groups of Lycra-clad friends drooling over the custom-made bikes, before cosying up on the chesterfields to reminisce about their best rides over steaming cups of coffee.

» Don't leave without asking the friendly staff about their dream ride. They're happy to advise on which cycle routes you should try out.

BAISIKELI

Map 2; Ingerslevsgade 103, Vesterbro; ///hairpin.staked.lobster; www.baisikeli.dk

This bike shop is perfectly located at the bottom of Dybbølsbro – Copenhagen's widest bike path – which connects to countless waterfront cycle paths. But it's not just the stellar location that makes checking out Baisikeli a no-brainer: it has a social conscience, too, with profits from its bike rentals and repairs going towards promoting cycling culture in Africa (*baisikeli* is Swahili for bicycle).

PEDALATLETEN

Map 4; Oslo Plads 9, Østerbro; ///renews.mimics.pushy; www.pedalatleten.dk

This rental shop prides itself on its varied selection of bikes. Choose from robust classics, romantic tandems, all-electric smooth operators or ubiquitous Christiania cargo bikes, then set off and explore Østerbro. We recommend tracing the Søerne (the lakes that bracket the city centre), which are just a quick pedal away.

WECYCLE

Map 5; Islands Brygge 21, Islands Brygge; ///laws.restriction.sketch; www.wecycle.dk

At WeCycle, two of the city's greatest loves – cycling and good coffee – come together. The bicycles are custom-made from scrap bike parts, making each one unique. And the coffee? It's just the thing for mulling your new set of wheels over.

KØBENHAVNS CYKELBØRS

Map 3; Gothersgade 157, Indre By; ///developer.singing.humans; www.cykelboersen.dk

Københavns Cykelbørs has been selling bikes since 1881, but this company is anything but old school. Admire the latest Raleigh bike and Nishiki touring model, then set off on a GPS-guided cycling tour to explore the city under your own steam and at your own pace.

» **Don't leave without** asking the friendly staff for tips on the rules of the road. Riding is easy, but there are still some things to bear in mind.

Liked by the locals

"Once you hop on your bicycle, side by side with mothers on cargo bikes carrying kids and the elderly just enjoying their morning ride, you realize that a cycling city is a human-sized city and that public space belongs to everyone."

ERDEM OVACIK, CEO OF BIKE-SHARING SERVICE DONKEY REPUBLIC

Street Style

Copenhageners are known for their cool style, but that doesn't mean that there's a uniform. Locals add a unique flair to their outfits, mixing chic and casual, sporty and dressy. Get the look at these stores.

GANNI

Map 1; Store Regnegade 12, Indre By; ///physics.bottled.drift; www.ganni.com

A byword for Scandi style, this Danish womenswear brand is known for its effortlessly cool designs. Do the printed dresses, funky jumpers and branded beanies in the flagship look familiar? With fashion influencers around the globe clamouring to become "Ganni girls", they've likely popped up on your social media feed.

ECOUTURE

Map 1; Læderstræde 5, Indre By; ///stress.invite.trainer; www.ecouture.com

It will come as no surprise that Ecouture's founder and owner, Johanne Helger Lund, was once a costume designer for film and television shows. Her theatrical, vintage-style designs represent all colours, eras and persuasions, and all of the garments are

On Fridays, Ecouture offers its customers a glass of bio bubbles, so you can sip while you browse.

sustainably and ethically produced. Think organic cotton dresses, eco-friendly leather bags and tights made from recycled nylon.

SIDEWALK SKATESHOP

Map 2; Enghave Plads 10, Vesterbro; ///slang.conclude.flown; www.sidewalkshop.dk

You'll catch many a skater screeching to a halt outside this shop, propping their board against the wall and adjusting their beanie, before popping in for the latest Thrasher tee or Vans shoes. Step inside to browse the skater-style gear, and then soak up some more street life by taking a seat on the bench outside, which is made of – you've guessed it – skateboards.

LOT#29

Map 4; Gothersgade 29, Indre By; ///ending.pegged.descended; www.lot29.dk

Mismatched rails of under-the-radar designer womens- and menswear, accessories randomly scattered on coffee tables and plenty of house plants: browsing in Lot#29 feels like you've stepped into the homes of owners and best friends Cecilie Kølpin and Line Hallberg. You'll even be offered a cup of tea while you rifle through the stock.

» **Don't leave without** taking a breath of fresh air – and sipping your tea – in the tiny garden out the back of the shop. You'll soon be joined by other shoppers or the impossibly friendly staff.

NAKED

Map 1; Klosterstræde 10, Indre By; ///shark.limo.probing; www.nakedcph.com

White trainers are a must-wear for many Copenhageners and Naked is *the* trainer shop for women looking to keep their footwear on point. Looking for a vintage pair? The sneaker-obsessed staff can tell you when and where the next pop-up, second-hand sneaker market will be held in the city.

MARIA BLACK

Map 1; Silkegade 13, Indre By; ///pricing.debater.chin; www.maria-black.com

Copenhageners are known for their pared-back style but that doesn't mean that they don't accessorize. And when locals are looking for the perfect piece to complete their outfit, a thoughtful birthday present or a last-minute anniversary gift, they hit up

Shh!

Hats might not be the first thing that comes to mind when you think of the Copenhagen street style scene, but Wilgart will soon change that *(www.wilgart.dk)*. Here, you'll find row upon row of flat caps, baseball caps, sailor hats and more. Owner Silas Gärtner learnt his trade from a master milliner in the Bavarian town of Bamberg before moving to Copenhagen, so the quality is unmatched and the designs are classic.

Danish-Irish designer Maria Black's jewellery store. Be warned: although pieces are surprisingly affordable, everything is designed to be stacked and layered, so it's hard to leave with just one thing.

LE FIX

Map 1; Kronprinsensgade 9, Indre By; ///struts.wiser.supper; www.le-fix.com

In 1999, three childhood friends who shared a love for art, tattoos and clothing got together and created this menswear brand specializing in hoodies, jeans and oversized shirts. After collaborations with Disney, record labels and FCK (Copenhagen's football club), Le Fix could be accused of becoming mainstream – but think again. This store's roots in underground culture run deep and continue to shape the design of both the products and the building itself (there's an art gallery on the top floor, and tattoo parlours and a wood workshop elsewhere)

» **Don't leave without** checking out the street art in surrounding Pisserenden – this is Indre By's edgiest corner.

RES-RES

Map 3; Guldbergsgade 29C, Nørrebro; ///blanked.logic.clearing; www.res-res.com

This store exemplifies – and fuels – Copenhageners' obsession with sustainability. Short for Respect Resources, Res-Res stocks an ethically sourced and eco-conscious version of just about anything you can think of: homeware, beauty products and accessories, as well as clothing for kids and adults. They even offer denim repairs so you never have to worry about parting with your favourite pair of jeans.

Book Nooks

Bookshops are cornerstones of their neighbourhoods, where children's first books (probably by Hans Christian Andersen) are bought and the local love of debate and discussion is fuelled.

TRANQUEBAR

Map 4; Borgergade 14, Indre By; ///spelled.tone.snapped; www.tranquebar.net

We admit it, we're biased, but it's hard to resist a bookshop dedicated to travel, adventure and escapism. Since it was established in 2006, Tranquebar has become the go-to destination for backpackers researching their next adventure and armchair travellers alike.

» **Don't leave without** asking to join the exclusive "reading lodge", which meets once a month to discuss a chosen book.

CAFÉ PALUDAN

Map 1; Fiolstræde 10, Indre By; ///mended.dearest.tested; www.paludan-cafe.dk

Denmark's oldest book café is where students come with good intentions to get group projects done, but end up discussing current events over mugs of hot chocolate instead. Beyond the double-height foyer and café, the bookshop has a library-like feel, with leather-bound treatises lining the towering wooden shelves.

BOOKS & COMPANY

Map 6; Sofievej 1, Hellerup; ///zoomed.people.swim; www.booksandcompany.dk

It's hard not to make friends at this English-language bookshop. The staff are friendly, the coffee corner is always buzzing with people who have long given up trying to read the latest *New York Times* bestseller and not one but seven different book clubs meet here each month.

ARK BOOKS

Map 3; Møllegade 10, Nørrebro; ///firmer.fatter.visit; www.arkbooks.dk

In 2013, two long-time volunteers at Literaturhaus were offered a teeny, tiny space to do something literary with. And after some crowdfunding (and calling in favours) these bookworms opened Ark – a non-profit bookshop that promotes international literature in translation.

Try it!

JOIN THE DISCUSSION

Community-run Literaturhaus hosts debates between critics, scholars and writers *(www.literaturhaus.dk)*. Check out the calendar and join groups of literature-loving friends at the next event.

CINNOBER BOOKSHOP

Map 1; Landemærket 9, Indre By; ///notices.maple.issuer; www.cinnoberbookshop.dk

If you're after a tome on Danish design to grace your coffee table, look no further than this carefully curated store. Here, you'll rub shoulders with budding designers, who come here eager for inspiration from the pages of the books and magazines.

THIEMERS MAGASIN

Map 2; Tullinsgade 24, Vesterbro; ///butter.examples.recount; www.thiemersmagasin.dk

With its red awning, blue façade and bright yellow floor, you'd be forgiven for thinking that Thiemers Magasin only stocked kids' books. But you'd be wrong – as well as picture books and fairytales, small-press novels, political volumes, self-help books and English classics all have a home here.

BOGHALLEN

Map 1; JP/Politikens Hus, Rådhuspladsen 37, Indre By; ///kitten.chains.letter; www.jppol.dk/boghallen/

Owned by the Danish newspaper *Politiken*, this is where the politically astute and culturally aware come to stock up on literature and listen to debates. At these regular events, well-known talking heads trade opinions on the latest contentious issues in current affairs.

» **Don't leave without** visiting the exhibition room, where you can enjoy a regularly updated collection of modern Danish art for free.

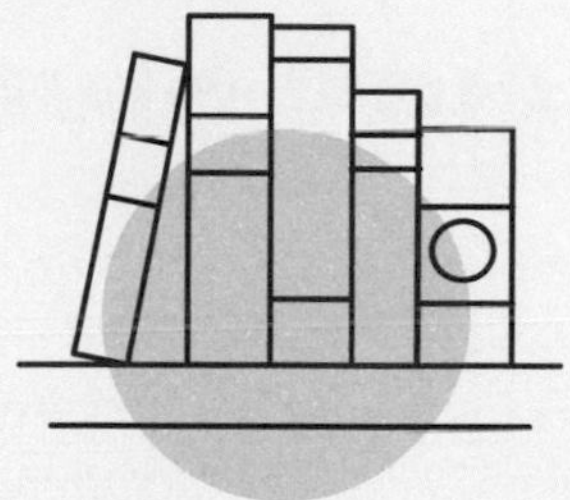

Liked by the locals

"Big chains can't really compete with indie bookshops. The staff are friendly, the shelves are made for browsing and there's often a little coffee corner where you can chat to a book-loving friend (and meet new ones, too)."

OLIVIA BURCHEA, BOOK LOVER AND DIGITAL CONTENT SPECIALIST AT LEGO

Record Stores

Put Spotify and iTunes aside for a minute. To keep it real, join Copenhagen's rockers and ravers, jazzheads and club kids between aisles of vinyl, swapping recommendations as you leaf through records.

BEAT

Map 2; Enghave Plads 13, Vesterbro;
///hesitate.groups.missing; www.beatcafe.dk

What do music fans love most about Beat? The eclectic selection of reasonably priced vinyl, which spans the gamut from psychedelia to country, jazz to electronica? The relaxing café with its enviable soundtrack? Or, perhaps, it's the selection of music literature (bonus: books are often in English). Whatever it is, it's enough to keep them coming back to this cosy nook time and time again.

SORT KAFFE & VINYL

Map 2; Skydebanegade 4, Kødbyen;
///outsiders.once.pushy; 61 70 33 49

When vinyl-collecting students fancy a laidback Sunday morning, they cycle over to this record store and café. Dressed in their casual vintage garms, they'll browse the small but special collection of new and reissued records, before ordering a freshly brewed coffee. Solo visitors, keen on listening to the background music (often from a rare 12-inch), sit on one of the stools inside while social pairs catch up on the pavement seats in the sun.

SOUND STATION

Map 2; Gammel Kongevej 94, Frederiksberg; ///comfort.provide.slings; www.soundstation.dk

Walking into Sound Station is like a trip down memory lane, with CDs, cassettes, squeaky VHS tapes and even some signed memorabilia all tightly packed in wooden bookcases and illuminated under warm lights. Locals who take the time to rifle through the stock here are rewarded with obscure rockabilly records and treasures from the punk era just waiting to be unearthed.

CRATE – BEER & VINYL

Map 3; Jægersborggade 50, Nørrebro; ///shop.educated.crystal; 22 81 77 08

One of those places that makes you ask, "Why did no one think of this sooner?", Crate is a record store and beer bar combo, where you can order a local brew and flip through a selection of new and classic records. As you might expect, this hybrid is a supremely social place, with regulars discussing their favourite discs over rounds of refreshing IPAs.

» **Don't leave without** checking with the staff when the next concert is; Crate often hosts intimate sets in-store.

ROUTE 66

Map 3; Fælledvej 3, Nørrebro; ///toenail.puzzled.clubs; 35 35 65 60

The place where locals come to stock up on their Danish music (think MØ, Trentemøller and Volbeat records), Route 66 also has a well-stocked selection of English-language records. For a deep dive into second-hand vinyl, descend the stairs to the basement, where you'll be crate-digging alongside Copenhagen's indie crowd.

SECOND BEAT ANTIKVARIAT

Map 3; Ryesgade 77, Østerbro; ///changes.stand.distract; www.secondbeat.dk

Second Beat is not just a wonderful place for dusty twelves from yesteryear; you'll also find all sorts of other second-hand gems, from quirky lamps to vintage comics. It all looks and feels like the

Shh!

Vinyl garage sales pop up in various locations across Copenhagen, offering the chance to get your hands on those hard-to-find albums. Folkehuset Absalon *(p44)* hosts a particularly good record market, specializing in indie genres, such as Baile funk, soul, disco, kwaito and trip hop. It's all the result of the tight-knit community of widely travelled DJs who sell their collections here. Keep tabs on Absalon's calendar so you don't miss out on a special sale.

living room of a culturally astute, but perhaps not very organized, old-timer. As a result, you could easily spend several hours here, rifling through records alongside keen collectors, bargain hunters and teenagers with an affinity for the 60s and 70s.

DORMA 21

Map 2; Oehlenschlægersgade 70, Vesterbro; ///communal.applied.glare; 71 61 87 49

This is your one-stop shop for electronic vinyl. No surprises then that it's a haven for techno heads, who rarely leave this basement without a record or two in the bag. Mosey around on a Friday or Saturday afternoon to find out where the weekend's best rave will go down (the owners and the folk that come here are usually well connected to the club scene).

BEAT BOP

Map 1; Fælledvej 3, Peder Hvitfeldts Stræde 12–16, Indre By; ///tones.pylon.resold; 33 15 93 19

Though run by heavy-metal legend Michael Denner, this no-frills vinyl trove doesn't just stock Denner's Mercyful Fate and King Diamond albums. Alongside the impressive metal collection, you'll find records, both niche and well-known, spanning all genres. Looking for some psych-rock vinyl? Denner's got it. Hunting for a rare live-show recording of The Doors? He might just have that, too.

» **Don't leave without** asking Denner for some of his favourite record recommendations.

An afternoon shopping in the **Latinerkvarteret**

Centred around Københavns Universitet, the Latin Quarter is so-called as Latin was the main language studied and spoken here until the early 1800s. Besides the many faculty buildings, this bustling part of town is one of the best places for budget-friendly shopping, with tons of cool vintage shops attracting eco-conscious students.

1. København K Charity Shop
Studiestræde 32, Latinerkvarteret; www.koebenhavnk.com ///clocked.chucks.study

2. The Living Room
Larsbjørnsstræde 17, Latinerkvarteret; www.thelivingroom.dk ///jazz.testing.rainy

3. Notre Dame
Nørregade 7, Latinerkvarteret; www.notredame.dk ///wished.freezing.soulful

4. Times Up Vintage
Krystalgade 4, Latinerkvarteret; www.timesupshop.com ///prompt.jaws.impaired

5. Danmission Op Shop
Rosengården 5, Latinerkvarteret; www.genbrug.danmission.dk ///indirect.these.passing

6. BRØG Litteraturbar
Fiolstræde 7, Latinerkvarteret; www.broeglitteraturbar.dk ///paradise.lavender.shocked

Gråbrødretorv *///sensual.exact.fracture*

Lunch at THE LIVING ROOM
Join the students in the cosy confines of this laid-back café. If you're here in the winter, try to bag a seat by the fireplace.

1

Rifle through KØBENHAVN CHARITY SHC
Walk down the alle to discover a treasu trove of uber-cool vintage clothes.

Hunt for a bargain at
DANMISSION OP SHOP

Finish your vintage shopping spree at this excellent charity shop. Inside, you'll find a mismatch of second-hand clothes and homewares.

Pick a book at
BRØG LITTERATURBAR

Beloved among literature-lovers, this book bar hosts author talks and regular readings. Pop by to pick up your next read and be sure to linger for a drink or two.

Stop by
TIMES UP VINTAGE

Follow fashionistas to quirky Times Up to browse the huge haul of vintage mens- and womenswear.

Browse homewares at
NOTRE DAME

Pick up some affordable Danish design gems – such as stylish clocks and timeless Scandi furniture – at Notre Dame. Lush house plants can be found here, too.

Hidden off the main drag, ***Gråbrødretorv*** *is a beautiful square lined with painted houses. It's a popular spot for students to hang out.*

ÅBENRÅ
5
FIOLSTRÆDE
NØRREGADE
P. HVITFELDTS STRÆDE
KØBMAGERGADE
LANDEMÆRKET
6
4
KRYSTALGADE
FIOLSTRÆDE
SKINDERGADE
LATINER-KVARTERET
GRÅBRØDRE-TORV
FRUE PLADS
STUDIESTRÆDE
3
AMAGERTORV
VESTERGADE
INDRE BY
NYTORV
0 metres 200
0 yards 200

ARTS & CULTURE

Copenhageners love a good debate. And the city's historic sights, forward-thinking architecture and innovative arts scene spark endless conversations.

City History

Cobbled alleys, beautiful palaces, rainbow-hued waterside houses: Copenhagen's history is palpable in the city's streets. Learn about the Copenhagen of yesteryear, today and tomorrow at these spots.

ASSISTENS KIRKEGÅRD

Map 3; Kapelvej 4, Nørrebro; ///parties.tutored.warmers; www.assistens.dk

Some of the biggest players in Danish history have been laid to rest in this rambling and romantic graveyard. Here lie the likes of writer Hans Christian Andersen, philosopher Søren Kierkegaard and rapper Natasja Saad. Yes, Copenhageners come here to feel humbled and inspired by their legacy, but this sacred ground is anything but sacrosanct. Locals read their books in quiet corners, share beers with friends and even steal kisses as they stroll through this green space.

BAKKEN

Map 6; Dyrehavevej 62, Klampenborg; ///retain.flows.depended; www.bakken.dk

Picture this: rolling rides, screams of ecstasy, the tantalizing whiff of Danish hot dogs. Welcome to Bakken, the world's oldest amusement park. Forget Tivoli – this is where funfairs first started way back in the 1500s, when folk flocked here for the spring water (the city centre's water was pretty gross at the time). Soon, enterprising stallholders set up trade, entertainers moved in – including Pjerrot the clown, who still performs today – and the amusement park was born.

» **Don't leave without** riding Rutschebanen, a wooden roller coaster still running as it did when it first opened in 1932.

AMALIENBORG

Map 4; Amalienborg Slotsplads, Indre By; ///insert.mopped.lemmings; www.kongernessamling.dk

Every schoolkid in Copenhagen is dragged around this palace at some point to brush up on royal Danish history (it's one of the oldest monarchies in the world, don't you know). And when they're all grown up, and have out-of-town friends or family visiting, they can't help but make a repeat visit. Swerving the uber-touristy changing of the guard, they make a beeline for the costume gallery and royal treasury to gawp at the beautiful dresses, brocaded uniforms and glittering crown jewels. Silver champagne cooler, anyone?

Try it!

PHOTOGRAPH HISTORY

Shooting Copenhagen runs photography workshops in the grounds of another palace, Rosenborg Slot. Here, you'll get your history fix while mastering the art of perspective *(www.shootingcopenhagen.com)*.

DANSK JØDISK MUSEUM

Map 5; Proviantpassagen 6, Indre By; ///teeth.reeling.mornings; www.jewmus.dk

How did 90 per cent of Denmark's Jewish population survive the Holocaust? The Danish Jewish Museum reveals all. It focuses on stories of the Jewish experience, including how the resistance coordinated the flight of over 7,000 Danish Jews to neutral Sweden in October 1943 – an uplifting moment in history.

LYKKEMUSEET

Map 4; Admiralgade 19, Indre By; ///partner.remover.flute; www.thehappinessmuseum.com

Denmark frequently tops the UN's annual World Happiness Report and now Danes are letting people in on their secrets. Spoiler alert: it's not all about hygge. The brainchild of the Copenhagen-based

Here's a lovely part of the city to wander around, away from the crowds. Kartoffelrækkerne was built in the late 19th century to provide hygienic workers' housing at the height of the cholera epidemic. And its socially minded architecture inspired later Danish builds such as Bjarke Ingels' 8 Tallet *(p130)*. Yes, gentrification may have transformed the apartments into sumptuous townhouses, but this little-visited part of Indre By is still infused with working-class history.

Happiness Research Institute, this small museum explores the geography, politics, history and future of happiness without being stuffy; smartphones, touching and talking are actively encouraged.

NYBODERS MINDESTUER

Map 4; Sankt Pauls Gade 24, Indre By; ///removal.narrow.adults; www.nybodersmindestuer.dk

While tourists trek out to Helsingør *(p185)* to learn about Copenhagen's maritime history, locals know they can stay closer to home. Located in the postcard-pretty neighbourhood of Nyboder (built in the 1630s to house Denmark's rapidly expanding navy) is this preserved sailors' home. Compasses, charts and even chamber pots are laid out as if the seasoned seafarers have just popped out for a stroll.

FREETOWN CHRISTIANIA

Map 5; Freetown Christiania; ///anchors.requested.restless

Okay, Freetown Christiania is in every guidebook. It's the pin-up for alternative thinking after all. But this is no human zoo – it's a place where people live, and Christianites are proud of their history. Once a semi-abandoned military base, this independent commune was founded in 1971 by disenfranchised residents of a nearby neighbourhood. Since then, Pusher Street's open hash market has given people certain preconceptions about the area but, make no mistake, this is a wonderland of communal living.

» **Don't leave without** joining a guided tour led by a long-time resident. Tours depart from the main entrance on Prinsessegade.

Favourite Museums

There are some museums that Copenhageners can't get enough of. And with such an incredible range of collections, frequently free admission and cool late-night openings, who can blame them?

LOUISIANA MUSEUM OF MODERN ART

Map 6; Gammel Strandvej 13, Humlebæk; ///stride.flatness.unload; www.louisiana.dk

The train from Copenhagen Central Station to the sleepy suburb of Humlebæk is always buzzing with creatives. They're bound for Denmark's beacon of contemporary art – Louisiana, which has hosted the likes of pumpkin-mad Yoyoi Kusama, climate-conscious Olafur Eliasson and pop artist David Hockney. If the ground-breaking

Try it!

LEARN TO PAINT

Fancy creating your own masterpiece? Book onto Louisiana's visual arts workshop, where an expert will teach you the techniques used by the artists on display *(www.louisiana.dk/en/whats-on/courses-workshops)*.

exhibitions inside weren't enough to convince Copenhageners to make the journey out to Humlebæk on the regular, then the peaceful sculpture garden has cemented the museum's popularity.

NY CARLSBERG GLYPTOTEKET

Map 5; Dantes Plads 7, Indre By; ///ladder.sizing.friday; www.glyptoteket.com

There are three things that Copenhageners love about Ny Carlsberg Glyptoteket (or the Glyptotek to its friends). First, the incredible collection of art amassed by brewer Carl Jacobsen (the Greek sculptures are a particular favourite). Second, the beautiful museum café, which is set in an atrium of towering palms. And third, the weekly special openings. (There's free admission on Tuesdays and extended hours on Thursdays.)

» Don't leave without checking out the *nasothek*. This intriguing collection is made up of the fake noses that were added to ancient Roman and Greek statues in the 19th century.

STATENS MUSEUM FOR KUNST

Map 3; Sølvgade 48–50, Indre By; ///fault.spoiler.canny; www.smk.dk

It's summertime, it's the weekend and you're in the mood for a classy but cool evening. Say hello to SMK, Denmark's largest art museum. On select Fridays this cultural powerhouse puts on an incredible show, tempting friends to start their weekend with a dose of culture that they'll muse on till Monday. Expect talks, screenings, music and even food trucks, all centred around the museum's incredible art collection.

Solo, Pair, Crowd

Whether you've got the day to yourself or you're exploring with the gang, there's a museum for you.

FLYING SOLO

Take a walk

In need of a bit of me-time? Dwell in the tranquil universe of French impressionism at Ordrupgaard Museum, before taking a contemplative stroll in the adjoining Art Park. The sculptures here are all nature-inspired.

IN A PAIR

A day out for two

Hop on the train to ARKEN – Louisiana's humbler sister – for a day of alternative modern art followed by a blustery walk along the nearby beach, where you can discuss what you've just seen.

FOR A CROWD

Pick an event

There's always something cool going on at the Kunsthal Charlottenborg exhibition centre. So, check the calendar, gather the gang and get ready for art fairs, literary talks, film festivals and more.

DESIGN MUSEUM DANMARK

Map 4; Bredgade 68, Indre By, ///pointer.nurture.popped; www.designmuseum.dk

Nestled amid the city's cool galleries and design firms, this museum has an effortlessly dressed crowd of regulars who wander over in their lunch hour. Join them as they check out the new exhibitions, browse the shop for last-minute birthday gifts and mull over their own creative ideas in the café.

» **Don't leave without** buying one of the iconic exhibition posters from the museum shop, so you can bring a bit of design home.

CISTERNERNE

Map 6; Bag Søndermarken, Frederiksberg; ///sweetly.burn.moped; www.cisternerne.dk

Subterranean water reservoirs are usually dark, dank and uninspiring places. Not so in Copenhagen. This converted cistern is one of the city's most atmospheric and conversation-provoking gallery spaces, hosting annual sound and light installations.

NATIONAL MUSEET

Map 1; Prinsens Palæ, Ny Vestergade 10, Indre By; ///unions.recruited.labels; www.natmus.dk

Dodging an inevitable rainy day? Make a beeline for the National Museum of Denmark. Everything you've ever wanted to know about Danish history can be found here, from the raiding days of the Vikings right up to the year 2000.

Top Theatres

Copenhagen's theatres are driven by the characteristics that define the city: a strong intellectual legacy and a critical point of view. And part and parcel of going to a performance here? Dissecting it in a bar afterwards.

BETTY NANSEN TEATRET

Map 2; Frederiksberg Allé 57, Frederiksberg; ///neat.rods.sailing; www.bettynansen.dk

Frederiksbergers fancy themselves as serious intellectuals, but this local theatre forces them to poke fun at themselves with its reinvented classics. Past productions have included a tongue-in-cheek performance of *A Midsummer Night's Dream* where the audience was encouraged to strip off to watch the show – we're not joking.

DET KONGELIGE TEATER

Map 4; August Bournonvilles Passage 2–8, Indre By; ///tipping.artist.foil; www.kglteater.dk

Copenhageners are, by and large, a casual bunch, known for their simple, utilitarian style. But there's one thing they'll shimmy into their glad rags for – the ballet. Come dusk, dressed-up Danes breeze through the doors of the Royal Danish Theatre's Old Stage to watch the pros pirouette and plié. Expect classics like *Romeo and Juliet* and the obligatory Christmas showing of *The Nutcracker*, as well as some surprising productions. *Come Fly Away*, for instance, used Frank Sinatra's crooning hits as the score.

BELLEVUE TEATRET

Map 6; Strandvejen 451, Klampenborg; ///unions.strategy.change; www.bellevueteatret.dk

Danish design has even infiltrated the world of theatre, and architect and furniture designer Arne Jacobsen is behind this functionalist build, with its bamboo-clad walls and retractable roof. On summer evenings, cuddled-up couples flock here to watch a musical, drama or satire under the stars. Once the curtain falls, they stroll hand in hand along nearby Bellevue beach, discussing the performance.

» Don't leave without going on a guided tour. You'll get a proper introduction to the history and architectural design of the theatre.

FOLKETEATRET

Map 1; Nørregade 39, Indre By; ///conclude.tooth.flags; www.folketeatret.dk

The People's Theatre is the oldest public theatre in Denmark and one that goes the extra mile to make its shows accessible to everyone (it even takes its productions on tour around the country so people outside of the city can get their theatre fix). Its wide variety of genres include classic plays, original productions and small-scale English-language performances, to name just a few.

WAREHOUSE9

Map 2; Halmtorvet 11A, Vesterbro; ///order.headache.just; www.warehouse9.dk

There are no genres – or boundaries – at this cross-disciplinary creative space. In fact, the only thing that Warehouse9's burlesque performances, poetry readings and film screenings have in common is that they present and promote LGBTQ+ perspectives. For many Vesterbroers the annual (and unmissable) *Queer Xmas Cabaret* show kick-starts their festive season.

BÅDTEATRET

Map 4; Nyhavn 16Z, Indre By; ///mule.blasted.zooms; www.baadteatret.dk

There's something very Copenhagen about watching experimental theatre aboard a boat moored in Nyhavn. Expect satire, re-interpreted works gone wonky and surprises left, right and centre in this playful

Shh!

Hidden in plain sight on Vesterbrogade, Teatret Ved Sorte Hest is a student favourite *(www.sortehest.com)*. Youngsters studying literature flock here to see their set texts brought to life on stage. Join them for a performance of Beckett, Ionesco or Pinter's famous works. Or – for something a bit different – sign up for an eye-opening lecture from brain researcher and TV personality Peter Lund Madsen.

world of puppet shows, cabarets and poetry readings. As it's located in tourist central, many performances are in English, but locals still come here to join the inevitable post-performance discussions.

» Don't leave without having a pre-theatre glass of wine at Niebbelo Winebar, which is just around the corner at Store Strandstræde 18.

BØSSEHUSET

Map 5; Mælkevejen 69D, Freetown Christiania; ///miles.nothing.baseline; www.boessehuset.dk

Known for queer storytelling with a universal appeal, this volunteer-run drama house has promoted inclusivity and acceptance since its founding in 1971. In classic Christiana style, members vote on the programme each week and there are regular pay-what-you-can performances and events (think naked yoga, "cuddle puddles" and raucous bingo nights).

TEATER REPUBLIQUE

Map 3; Østerfælled Torv 37, Østerbro; ///shut.victor.words; www.osterbroteater.dk/teater-republique

Got an appetite for the avant-garde? Bring nothing but an open mind to Teater Republique, which shows dramas by the likes of absurdist Bertolt Brecht. On top of existential plays, the theatre hosts battling magicians, underwater dance shows and immersive dining experiences. Past performances have included a dramatization of Karen Blixen's short story *Babette's Feast*, accompanied by the food served in the tale (minus the turtle soup, of course).

Indie Galleries

Copenhagen has a long tradition of free speech and liberalism, especially when it comes to art. From provocative photography to evocative prints, anything goes in the ever-changing indie art scene.

BORCH

Map 6; Prags Boulevard 49, Amager; ///outlined.cities.sourced; www.borcheditions.com

Printmaking is the focus at this studio-shop, with owner and print master Niels Borch Jensen imparting his wisdom to a clique of enterprising apprentice artists. The shop floor itself is one big workshop, where the genesis of an idea and the final product walk hand in hand in one cluttered heap of tools, prints and paint stains. But among the mess are masterpieces – and affordable ones, too.

MARTIN ASBÆK GALLERY

Map 4; Bredgade 23, Indre By; ///waitress.daring.passing; www.martinasbaek.com

Leading the charge for the photographic arts in Denmark, Martin Asbæk is on a mission to promote Nordic photographers on the global stage, and regularly opens pop-up galleries at international art fairs. As such, this trailblazing gallery is a creative hub for all things photographic: exhibitions, yes, but also talks and events with Copenhagen's glittorati.

» Don't leave without ducking into nearby Oscar's to reflect on the photography while tucking into the scrumptious smørrebrød. This LBGTQ+ bar and café's Friday night DJ sets always draw an arty crowd.

GALLERI KBH KUNST

Map 3; Øster Søgade 34, Indre By; ///rejects.pins.stubble; www.kbhkunst.dk

Looking to find the next big artist? Look no further. Located on the corner of artistic haven Rørholmsgade, this gallery is dedicated to fostering hot, new talent. Owner Helle Borre even offers two on-site studio spaces to up-and-coming artists who don't have the luxury of room at home. Expect brightly coloured paintings, bronzes and ceramic sculptures, and buzzing exhibition openings.

We'd include all the artist-owned galleries on relatively unknown Rørholmsgade here if we could *(www.roerholmsgade.com)*. Over 25 diverse artists – from watercolourists to glass blowers – are part of this closely knit street collective. Its small studios, galleries and workshops are only open to the public on the first Sunday afternoon of each month, but you can book an appointment to visit at other times, too.

NIKOLAJ KUNSTHAL

Map 1; Nikolaj Plads 10, Indre By; ///curtains.ends.tasters; www.nikolajkunsthal.dk

It may be housed within a church, but that's as far as this gallery's piety goes. In fact, Nikolaj Art Centre's innuendo-riddled exhibitions, provocative talks and late-night opening parties are designed to challenge Denmark's religious and civic values.

COPENHAGEN CONTEMPORARY

Map 4; Refshalevej 173A, Refshaleøen; ///ends.lonely.cabinet; www.copenhagencontemporary.org

Creatives sporting steel-rimmed spectacles and well-worn Dr Martens flock to this welding factory-turned-gallery to pass judgment on the latest cutting-edge contemporary installations. Think provocative videos, messy stencils and colliding colours.

» **Don't leave without** walking or biking around Refshaleøen while you're here. This post-industrial wasteland has its own artistic quality.

GALLERI OXHOLM

Map 6; Pile Allé 25, Frederiksberg; ///comment.siblings.musician; www.gallerioxholm.dk

Although it's located in respectable and upmarket Frederiksberg, Oxholm is anything but conservative. The gallerists are very responsive to current affairs, so expect hot takes on anything political or controversial here – often in the form of oil on canvas, with a dash of surrealism for good measure.

Liked by the locals

"Copenhagen's art scene is living and breathing. Luckily for art lovers, this means that you're never far away from a mind-opening exhibition. Increasingly, drinks, a DJ and food have become synonymous with Friday evening exhibition launches."

ANNE-SOPHIE MEISNER, ART HISTORIAN

Contemporary Architecture

There's no need to venture inside to discover the cutting-edge. This city is one big gallery and its modern buildings are the art works. And like all good art, these builds divide opinion, earning both fans and critics.

BLOX

Map 5; Bryghuspladsen, Indre By; ///gently.surfaces.notion; www.blox.dk

We couldn't not mention Blox, the home of the Danish Architecture Centre (DAC) and a building that's been provoking debate since its foundations were laid. Some say it looks like any old office block, with its green-tinted glass and metal grilles, while others hail this

Try it!

JOIN THE DISCUSSION

The DAC hosts debates and talks on the big issues facing contemporary buildings. Sign up and learn about sustainable cities, green transport and Nordic design, before forming your own opinions.

multi-disciplinary space as a city in miniature. The DAC also sparks discussions about Copenhagen's other contemporary constructions through its exhibitions, talks and walking tours. Take in the builds, listen to your guide and then join in the debate.

CYKELSLANGEN

Map 2; access via Dybbølsbro, Vesterbro; ///bearings.boomed.wool

A bike-mad city requires safe and continuous cycling infrastructure. Enter Cykelslangen, an elevated cycle highway that has commuters zipping over Sydhavnen harbour in no time at all. But why would you want to rush this sci-fi scenic ride? Meandering between glass buildings before snaking high above the harbour, this bright orange asphalt ribbon is as beautiful as it is practical.

» Don't leave without cycling further along the water to Cirkelbroen. Danish Icelandic artist Olafur Eliasson is behind this boat-like bridge.

COPENHILL

Map 4; Vindmøllevej 6, Amager; ///rash.measures.dine; www.copenhill.dk

Even power plants have been given the Danish design treatment in Copenhagen. An operational waste-to-energy power plant with the serious mission of contributing to the city's carbon-neutral goal, CopenHill is also an outdoor playground. This urban mountain has the world's highest climbing wall scaling one side of its steel façade and a verdant ski piste and hiking trail on its roof. Pros cruise down the slope, while après-ski lovers – who choose snowballs over snowploughs – soak up the vibe over drinks at the café.

TIETGENKOLLEGIET

Map 5; Rued Langgaards Vej 10, Islands Brygge; ///darkens.uptown.vocally; www.tietgenkollegiet.dk

Affectionately dubbed "The Colosseum" by the students lucky enough to inhabit it, the Tietgen Residence Hall looks a bit like an ancient stadium, with its Jenga-like apartments encircling a central courtyard. This open-air atrium is the building's heart, where residents and guests lounge and socialize. It all feels very communal, especially when the grand piano is wheeled out into the courtyard from the music room for alfresco performances. We wish we lived here, and so will you.

8 TALLET

Map 6; Richard Mortensens Vej, Islands Brygge; ///benched.reward.wires; www.8tallet.dk

How did this structure earn the name "8 House", you ask? It's more obvious when you see its bow-shaped living roof from above. Walk the moss-sedum ramps to the top, admiring the building's design and the mist-blurred, prairie-like landscape of Amagerfælled beyond, before coming back down to earth with a coffee from the ground-floor café. Guided tours are available Monday to Saturday.

OPERAEN

Map 4; Ekvipagemestervej 10, Christianshavn; ///weep.stepping.compiled; www.kglteater.dk

Opera singers harness a deep-bellied power to support their voices, and this opera house seems to have been inspired by its performers.

Aged between 15 and 30? Sign up to Young Opera for discounted tickets, and money off food and drinks.

With its curvaceous glass façade and overhanging flat roof, the exterior has a rotund appearance, while the sunken auditorium seems almost womb-like.

SKUESPILHUSET

Map 4; Sankt Annæ Plads 36, Indre By; ///vehicle.cool.define; www.kglteater.dk

With its jutting glass overhang, the Royal Danish Playhouse is not dissimilar to the Operaen, which it faces across the water. But if the opera house represents the comforting hygge of the winter months, Skuespilhuset is firmly rooted in the summer, when people picnic on the sun-soaked, wrap-around terrace (40 per cent of the building sits on stilts over the harbour).

KONDITAGET LÜDERS

Map 6; Helsinkigade 30, Nordhavn; ///pulled.rides.drainage; 33 76 98 00

We imagine that car parks are pretty boring buildings to design. Not so to infrastructure specialists JAJA Architects, who definitely had fun when they came up with this car park-meets-playground. Konditaget Lüders' roof is dotted with monkey bars, swings and trampolines that kids play on with reckless abandon and adults use to work out – when they can tear themselves away from the views of Copenhagen Harbour, that is.

» **Don't leave without** taking in the silo – a futuristic pearl of a building on the opposite side of the street.

Public Art

Copenhagen's subversive, free-thinking and politically engaged character runs deep, and this is no more evident than in the murals and sculptures that punctuate the urban turf.

WESTEND

Map 2; Vesterbrogade 65–78, Vesterbro; ///modest.transmit.eating

In 1901, this section of Vesterbrogade was intended to house sex workers, but two years later prostitution was made illegal. Instead, theatre folk moved in and kick-started Westend's legacy of creative expression. Local artists bomb the street's arched entrance on a weekly basis, creating an ever-changing art gallery that perfectly captures the rebellious nature of modern street art and Copenhagen itself.

BANANNA PARK

Map 3; Nannasgade 4, Nørrebro; ///legend.soils.submits; www.kobenhavnergron.dk

What was once the toxic soil beneath an old oil refinery now grows green, and locals flock to BaNanna Park for picnics, football games and the climbing wall. But you're here for the street art. The arched entrance is scaled by a stencilled gorilla; cartoon characters frolic on a façade beside moody, black-and-white portraits; and Christian Hansen's towering *Yggdrasil* dominates one wall. Depicting the sacred tree from Norse cosmology, this work sums up the park's MO: nature will triumph if it's given the chance.

» Don't leave without walking over to Dea Trier Mørch's mural on nearby Stefansgade. On a brilliant blue background, Mørch has painted evocative lines from a poem by Inger Christensen.

PRINSESSEGADE

Map 5; Prinsessegade, Christianshavn; ///jokes.cursing.diagram

You'd be forgiven for cruising past the long line of murals on this unassuming street on your way to Christiania. But take it slow and you'll notice how a few tags on Christianshavn's stately walls evolve into a splattered graffiti gallery. Locals can't resist biking by to see what's new – like an unbelievably lifelike, spray-painted portrait of local rock legend Kim Larsen, who died in 2018.

When the City Circle Line was being constructed between 2011 and 2019, local artists were commissioned to paint murals on the hoardings. It became a fantastic temporary urban gallery that many locals still miss. Luckily enough, an extension of the line to Sydhavnen is still being built (projected for completion in 2024) and new graffiti is popping up each day. Head to the area behind the Belvederekanalen to find it.

FREETOWN CHRISTIANIA

Map 5; Freetown Christiania; ///rent.corner.applause

The nexus of Copenhagen's countercultural spirit, Freetown Christiania *(p115)* is home to some of the city's best and most politicized urban art. Think comments on the police's treatment of ethnic minorities and Banksy-influenced portraits of the homeless.

» Don't leave without heading over to Café Månefiskeren for a strong cup of coffee among Christianites.

BOLSJEFABRIKKEN

Map 6; Ragnhildgade 1, Østerbro; ///revised.length.because; www.bolsjefabrikken.com

The Candy Factory defies labels. It's an abandoned warehouse, a community, a counter-cultural organization, a non-profit, a music venue, an art gallery – the list goes on. And the murals that adorn Bolsjefabrikken's walls are just as difficult to pin down. We can't really describe what artworks to expect here as they change constantly, but you can bet on seeing some bold and beautiful graffiti.

THE GREAT STORY OF THE LITTLE PEOPLE AND THE GIANT TROLLS

Map 5; start at Sydområdet 30, Freetown Christiana; ///dove.helpers.cycles; www.thomasdambo.com

Traipse around Copenhagen and you'll spot a whole horde of "giants". This is no coincidence; created from scrap wood by Thomas Dambo and a host of local volunteers, and located in

We'll give you a helping hand to find your first giant. One of them *(Green George)* is in Christiania.

scenic but overlooked spots, this project aims to get families out discovering and enjoying nature. Check out the map online to locate the giants (hint: head west).

FØDDER MØDES

Map 3; Griffenfeldsgade 44, Nørrebro; ///reacting.staring.slurs; www.carolinethon.com

On an ageing building in a quaint corner of Nørrebro, you'll see something that looks like a faded Dalí mash-up gone wild. Created by local artist Caroline Thon in 2019, *Meeting Feet* combines the "foot portraits" of 84 Nørrebroers. Thon believes that our feet reveal where we've come from and her website tells the story behind each sole.

THE GENETICALLY MODIFIED LITTLE MERMAID

Map 4; Langelinie Allé 17, Østerbro; ///conned.risky.pocket

Everyone wants to see Edvard Eriksen's famous bronze, *The Little Mermaid*, but it's nearly always a disappointment. Instead, seek out Bjørn Nørgaard's sculpture for something that'll spark debate and have you seeing things differently. A critique of modern society's obsession with beauty and reliance on GM foods, *The Genetically Modified Little Mermaid* has a misshapen head and wonky limbs. Like her or not, she'll likely leave an impression, which is not usually the case with her sister. And, since beauty is in the eye of the beholder, we'll let you be the judge of which is the fairest of them all.

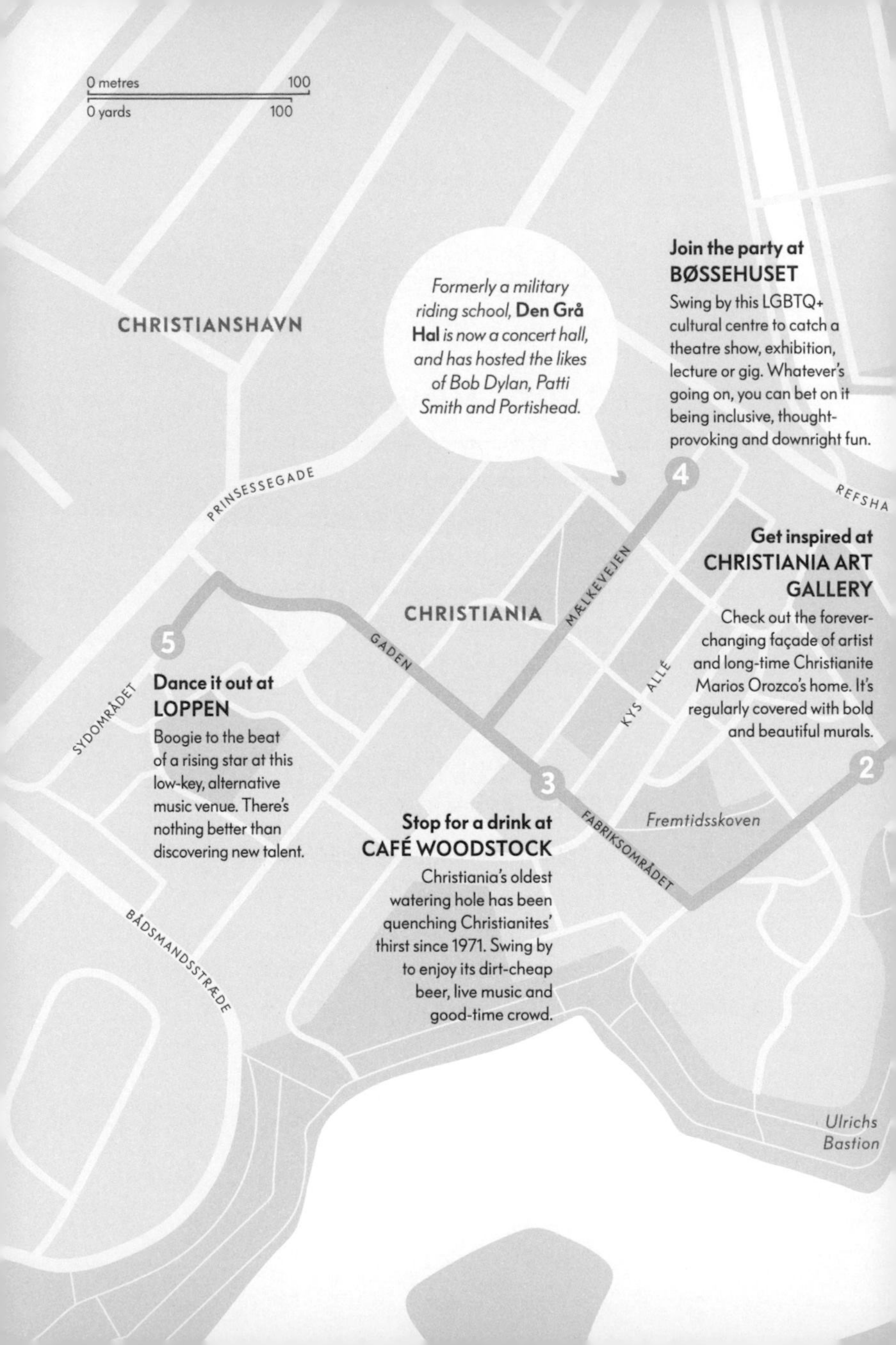

0 metres 100
0 yards 100

CHRISTIANSHAVN

Formerly a military riding school, **Den Grå Hal** *is now a concert hall, and has hosted the likes of Bob Dylan, Patti Smith and Portishead.*

Join the party at
BØSSEHUSET

Swing by this LGBTQ+ cultural centre to catch a theatre show, exhibition, lecture or gig. Whatever's going on, you can bet on it being inclusive, thought-provoking and downright fun.

4

PRINSESSEGADE

REFSHA

Get inspired at
CHRISTIANIA ART GALLERY

Check out the forever-changing façade of artist and long-time Christianite Marios Orozco's home. It's regularly covered with bold and beautiful murals.

MÆLKEVEJEN

CHRISTIANIA

5

GADEN

Dance it out at
LOPPEN

Boogie to the beat of a rising star at this low-key, alternative music venue. There's nothing better than discovering new talent.

SYDOMRÅDET

KYS ALLÉ

2

3

FABRIKSOMRÅDET

Fremtidsskoven

Stop for a drink at
CAFÉ WOODSTOCK

Christiania's oldest watering hole has been quenching Christianites' thirst since 1971. Swing by to enjoy its dirt-cheap beer, live music and good-time crowd.

BÅDSMANDSSTRÆDE

Ulrichs Bastion

An evening of counter-culture in **Christiania**

It may have earned a reputation for its relaxed residents (and equally laissez-faire approach to marijuana), but don't underestimate the force of Freetown Christiania's cultural scene. The alternative spirit of the pioneers who set up this commune back in the 1970s as a protest against the city's lack of affordable housing lives on. You'll find it in Christiania's politically engaged street art, lively music venues and community spaces, where locals come to set the world to rights.

1. Morgenstedet
Fabriksområdet 134, Freetown Christiania; www.morgenstedet.dk
///strut.amuse.profile

2. Christiania Art Gallery
Fabriksområdet 94A, Freetown Christiania; www.christianiaart.dk
///unravel.dollar.oblige

3. Café Woodstock
Mælkevejen 87, Freetown Christiania; www.cafe-woodstock.business.site
///denote.areas.unto

4. Bøssehuset
Mælkevejen 69D, Freetown Christiania; www.boessehuset.dk
///miles.nothing.baseline

5. Loppen
Sydområdet 4B, Freetown Christiania; www.loppen.dk
///chase.embodied.listed

Copenhagen Victory Stupa
///riches.maximum.gain

Den Grå Hal
///envy.noble.shopper

Built in 2019, the **Copenhagen Victory Stupa** *symbolizes and reflects Christianites' deep-rooted spirituality.*

FABRIKSOMRÅDET

Fuel up at
MORGENSTEDET
Tuck into hearty vegan cooking at this no-frills restaurant. It's volunteer-run, so the cook (and menu) changes daily. PS you're expected to clear your own table when you've finished.

Stadsgraven

NIGHTLIFE

Copenhagen's understated character extends to its nightlife scene. Friends catch up in* hyggelig *brown bars and couples cuddle up in intimate jazz cafés to watch musicians play.

Cool Clubs

Though locals often prefer an intimate party, this city still has a few big clubs for the ravers. Whether you're looking for a living-room-size gathering gone wild or a hardcore techno cave, Copenhagen's got you covered.

THE JANE

Map 1; Gråbrødretorv 8, Indre By;
///holidays.singers.plugged; www.thejane.dk

A night at The Jane is like a Jay Gatbsy party: bartenders whip up Prohibition-style cocktails, stylish wood panels line the walls and moody lighting illuminates the well-dressed crowd of revellers. The party really begins late at night (see, Gatsby really would approve) so play it cool, and don't expect to get in if you're slurring your words.

MESTEREN & LÆRLINGEN

Map 2; Flæsketorvet 86, Vesterbro;
///dwell.welfare.swarm; 32 15 24 83

If, like many a Copenhagener, funk 'n' soul gets you in your groove, head to this laidback haunt. It's a popular pre-drink spot, but we wouldn't blame you if you ended up staying the whole night – it's happened to the best of us. Funky tunes blast from the tiny DJ booth

Start here before ending the evening at Jolene – a short walk away. Both are usually free to enter.

while an intimate crowd of hipsters and Vesterbro locals let loose. Bring your gang, order some cheap beers and get ready for a night to remember.

JOLENE BAR

Map 2; Flæsketorvet 81–85, Kødbyen; ///safest.silent.rescuer; www.jolene.dk

Jolene is the incarnation of the Meatpacking District's nightlife scene: groovy music, a closely packed dance floor and a bunch of friendly revellers. Locals of all tribes (Jolene welcomes, and truly embraces, everyone) turn up on a Friday night ready to sweat, smile and dance to classic disco and deep house under colourful lights and disco balls.

» Don't leave without **doing as the locals do and grabbing a Jägerbomb at the bar once you've hung your coat up. The rest is history.**

ZEFSIDE

Map 1; Frederiksholms Kanal 4, Indre By; ///riot.package.translated; www.zefside.dk

Delicious drinks, seemingly endless happy hours – 2-for-1 cocktail offers can last for six hours some nights, so pace yourself – and top-notch DJs make Zefside a go-to for young guns when the weekend hits. Rock up early if you want to make the most of the cheap drinks but don't tap out too soon: DJ sets and dance floor antics only get better as the night unfurls.

CULTURE BOX

Map 4; Kronprinsessegade 54, Indre By; ///roofer.shelve.solve; www.culture-box.com

With its strobe lights and irresistible DJ beats, this cooler-than-cool club gives off all the vibes of a Berlin nightclub. The Box was one of the city's very first electronic music hubs, so it's a rite of passage for techno heads and wannabe DJs who rock up here on a Friday night. Expect high-quality tunes spanning house, techno and drum 'n' base, and top-of-the-range speakers that keep clubbers' ears ringing till dawn.

RUST

Map 3; Guldbergsgade 8, Nørrebro; ///fizzle.rate.accent; www.rust.dk

During the week, this versatile venue hosts up-and-coming indie rock bands and hip hop artists (though famous faces like Flight Facilities occasionally grace the stage here). But on Friday and Saturday nights (and the occasional wild weekday), the city's best disc spinners rule over two different dance floors – the airy main room and the edgy, if slightly dank, basement. Join the energetic students and get ready to party hard.

CLUB MAMBO

Map 1; Vester Voldgade 83-85, Indre By; ///misfits.hints.scar; www.clubmambo.dk

Looking for a fun-filled fiesta rather than a night of heavy techno? Club Mambo's got your back. Whether you're into Latin, pop or reggaeton music, this Latin club will always get you dancing (no matter how sober you are). Speaking of dancing, if you're looking to brush up on your skills before the evening starts, attend one of Club Mambo's salsa lessons – they're almost as fun as a night at the club.

BREMEN

Map 2; Nyropsgade 39–41, Indre By; ///entire.lamps.staked; www.brementeater.dk

A theatre by day, a party by night, Bremen enjoys every minute of its shape-shifting personality. Come dusk, you'll find this popular venue shedding its family-friendly skin for strobe lights and strong drinks as an eager crowd of clubbers line up outside for hours (embrace the wait – you might make some new friends). Once in, descend the steps, buy a round and you'll be dancing to pop music all night long.

» Don't leave without sipping one of Bremen's refreshing yet cheap cocktails, all of which are served in cute jars

You won't find much going on in the outskirts of Nørrebro after dark – that is, until you stumble upon the queue for Sigurdsgade *(info@sigurdsgade.com)*. Hidden away in the suburbs, this buzzing venue is still unbeknown to some locals. It's notorious among the city's rave crowd though, who turn up every weekend for Sigurdsgade's massive parties (think epic disco marathons and underground DJ sets). If rave culture's your jam, be sure to add this one to your bucket list.

Brown Bars

Locals love their brown bars. They epitomize what a* hyggelig *night out is all about: cheap beer, card games, conversations with strangers and a good sing-along, all in dimly lit confines.

EIFFEL BAR

Map 5; Wildersgade 58, Christianshavn; ///unusually.turkey.edit; www.eiffelbar.dk

Nestled in the narrow backstreets of old Christianshavn, this Parisian-style hang-out draws a diverse crowd. It's mellow during the day, with aged locals and intellectuals nursing their drinks and chatting quietly. Come the evening, young office workers cram around the tables, exclaiming over drinking games, loudly clinking their beer bottles and downing shots with the bar staff.

JAGUAR BODEGA

Map 5; Holmbladsgade 12, Amager; ///lungs.magical.writers; 32 57 06 87

Want to unlock the city's secrets? Strike up a conversation with one of the eccentric locals in this old-timey bar. Here, yarns are spun between sips of beer and the tall-tale tellers are all too eager to impart their wit to newcomers – the regulars have heard it all before, twice. Some things have changed over the years – there's now a no-smoking policy, so you can actually see the people you're talking to – but lots has stayed the same. The beer's still cheap and the walls, once hidden behind clouds of smoke, show the tobacco stains of the past.

MC. KLUUD

Map 2; Istedgade 126, Vesterbro;
///nodded.veers.rafters; www.mckluud.dk

If you'd have rocked up at this western-themed bar in the 70s, nights might have turned a little dodgy – Mc. Kluud's was a favourite among biker gangs. Nowadays, it's a student hang-out; catch them challenging each other to billiards while nodding to old rock tunes on the jukebox.

» Don't leave without ordering a classic brown ale. Regulars will tell you the brown ale here tastes better than it does in any other brown bar.

CAFE MALMØ

Map 4; Havnegade 35, Indre By;
///welcome.respond.fatter; 33 12 72 60

When every other bar in Indre By is closed, party-goers stumble down the stairs to this final frontier. Admittedly, it's a little dingy, but it's got character: tables are dressed in chequered cloths and walls are lined from top to bottom with every kind of bottle top and raggle-taggle trinket. Inside you'll meet woozy clubbers and tough-looking Danes banging their beer mugs together and shouting *"skål!"* like they're the best of friends.

Liked by locals

"As my aunt Cindy (the previous owner) used to say, the guests at Café Sommersted behave well because she raised them well! I guess she must be right, as there's always a great atmosphere here – even well into the wee hours of the morning."

JENNY FANG, OWNER OF CAFÉ SOMMERSTED

CAFÉ SOMMERSTED

Map 2; Sommerstedgade 2, Vesterbro; ///opinion.lifts.grills; 91 87 86 89

A legendary local staple, Café Sommersted is the kind of place you'll leave having made a new friend or two. Take Jenny, the owner, who is just as friendly to newcomers that wind up here as she is with the lively regulars who have called this watering hole their second home for years. It's super close to the Meatpacking District clubs, too, so there's never a dull crowd, nor a dull moment.

» Don't leave without ordering a tasty croque-monsieur sandwich from the bar– they're a speciality here.

BO-BI BAR

Map 1; Klareboderne 14, Indre By; ///circle.muddle.farms; 33 12 55 43

If you're looking for the lowdown on Danish politics, head on over to this legendary establishment, founded by a sailor in 1917. It's a favourite among journalists and impassioned political students, who come here regularly for a friendly debate over a bottle of beer.

FUNCHS VINSTUE

Map 3; Nørre Farimagsgade 55, Indre By; ///safely.tablets.shiver; 33 11 54 45

Vinstue might mean wine bar in Danish but, as with most brown bars, it's all about cheap beer here. Couples mull over games of chess (which may well be paused and restarted on their next visit) while groups of students slouch across the chunky leather sofas for hours on end.

Live Music

People from all walks of life gather in Copenhagen's live music venues, all looking to be carried away by the music. And with everything from techno DJ sets to blues concerts, there's something new to discover each night.

OPERAEN CHRISTIANIA

Map 5; Christianshavn; ///along.grunge.dine; 32 57 29 09

Operaen lives and breathes the spirit of Freetown Christiania. Within its alternative interior, you'll spot modern-day Charlie Chaplin-esque eccentrics, students with a few coins left in their pockets and creatives keen on counter-culture immersion. They're here for the world music acts and other obscure treasures of the musical deep – don't expect any famous faces at this hideout.

KIND OF BLUE

Map 3; Ravnsborggade 17, Nørrebro; ///touches.clips.trainer; www.kindofblue.dk

This blues bar looks and feels like a Danish living room from a 1970s design catalogue – think bold blue walls and cool designer furniture. Step inside and you'll spot casually dressed friends and first dates, just inches apart at the candlelit tables as they listen to the soothing sounds of live blues. Don't fret if you've turned up solo though – owner and music-buff Claus Ploug can invariably be found at the bar and he's always up for a chat.

VEGA

Map 2; Enghavevej 40, Vesterbro; ///closes.inform.kindest; www.vega.dk
Once called the "Sistine Chapel at Vesterbro", this architectural gem was originally the meeting place for the city's labour movement. Previous patrons, who dined and discussed politics under stylish hanging lamps in the wood-panelled hall, might be surprised to discover their turf is now ruled by energetic concert-goers. The iconic features remain, though, serving as an atmospheric backdrop for live performances of all genres.

» **Don't leave without** catching one of Draghouse's (a drag queen company) iconic shows. They're the stuff of local legend.

Extreme and experimental shows – the sort of thing that proves punk is not dead – are the order of the day at Mayhem *(www.mayhemkbh.dk)*. This cool customer keeps a very low profile when it comes to promotion, so it's still shrouded in a good dose of mystery. It's part of Bolsjefabrikken ("The Candy Factory", an alt-culture house run by an autonomous community) and much like the rest of this creative bonanza, the outside is covered in layer upon layer of ever-changing street art *(p134)*.

Solo, Pair, Crowd

Many a night in Copenhagen involves live music. Whatever company you keep, you're bound to find a spot to suit.

FLYING SOLO

One with the music

Don't miss the street art at the entrance of Spillestedet Stengade, a temple of sound in Nørrebro. Inside, the black walls of this volunteer-run concert hall are an apt spot to lose yourself in the underground music.

IN A PAIR

A classy couple

Walk hand in hand by the sea near Islands Brygge before a classical music concert at Mogens Dahl Koncertsal. Expect a sophisticated evening of chamber music – perfect for that special anniversary celebration.

FOR A CROWD

Alice in mosh pit land

Alice is a Nørrebro nook that serves up a mix of experimental and world music. Hold on to your mates and get ready for a (fairly controlled) mosh pit.

PUMPEHUSET

Map 2; Axelorv 8, Vesterbro; ///freed.lots.diet; www.pumpehuset.dk

Yes, Pumpehuset puts on some epic gigs for fans of alternative music. But its outdoor garden, Byhaven (open in the warmer months), is what we really want to shout about. Alfresco concerts here are free and the crowd – largely après-work drinkers and students – is always buzzing.

TJILLI POP

Map 3; Rantzausgade 28, Nørrebro; ///dearest.quickly.rail; 35 35 90 20

When Copenhagen's students finish for the day, they head to Tjilli Pop for a chilled one. Vintage furniture and a messy arrangement of wall items – from broken banjos to a wonderfully wonky chandelier that looks like it'll fall down at any moment – create an informal atmosphere inside this kooky joint. Meanwhile, local singer-songwriter acts take to the stage, cheered on by their friends and brand new fans.

» **Don't leave without** trying out the open mic. You probably won't find a more encouraging crowd anywhere else in the city.

CAFÉ NEMOLAND

Map 5; Fabriksområdet 52, Christianshavn; ///home.snuggles.exposes; www.nemoland.dk

You might mistake this music venue for an abandoned site if you pass it in winter. Amble over in the summer, though, and it's a whole other story. Hordes of revellers, sporting their latest vintage garms, sip cheap beer and sway to reggae and hip hop acts, pleasantly cooled by the breeze from the nearby lakes. Talk about idyllic.

LGBTQ+ Scene

Ever-tolerant and ever-vibrant, Copenhagen's LGBTQ+ scene is world-famous. You'll be welcomed with open arms at a number of inclusive venues and nightlife spots across this friendly city.

CENTRALHJØRNET

Map 1: Kattesundet 18, Indre By; ///stables.hill.monument; 33 11 85 49

Copenhagen's oldest LGBTQ+ bar is as laidback as they come. If you're after a messy night, keep walking. But if you're looking for a casual pint and a friendly atmosphere, make this your home for the evening. The easy-going bar staff greet you like you've been coming here for years, as many of the regulars have – expect an older crowd, who'll probably call you over to join their table as the night goes on.

» **Don't leave without** enjoying a chilled evening pint outside on one of the pavement tables (hopefully in the sunshine).

VELA GAY CLUB

Map 2; Viktoriagade 2, Vesterbro; ///violin.scatter.stiff; www.velagayclub.dk

Step inside Copenhagen's only exclusively lesbian bar (though allies are always welcome) and you're likely to be roped in to join one of the beer pong or table football competitions. Bar games not your

Keep an eye on Vela's events calendar – it often hosts live music, speed dating and poetry readings.

thing? Join the more low-key regulars sipping sweet cocktails and flirting in the corner. A few drinks down, the intimate dance floor is hard to resist.

G*A*Y COPENHAGEN

Map 1; Vester Voldegade 10, Indre By; ///restricts.ranks.avoiding; 33 14 13 30

Not even a global pandemic could dampen this bar's love of drag: performances moved online during the city's lockdown. Aside from G*A*Y's constant stream of drag shows, expect a fun-loving crowd of LGBTQ+ folk and their friends letting loose on the busy (and sweaty) dance floor. Throwback disco tunes and mainstream chart-toppers are the go-to here, as is shameless, hands-in-the-air boogying.

JAILHOUSE CPH

Map 1; Studiestræde 12, Indre By; ///survive.cotton.garage; www.jailhousecph.dk

Everyone's had a night to remember at G*A*Y's sister bar and enjoyed telling the tales. Copenhagen's ultimate bad-decision gay bar, this kinky joint has windows lined with jail bars and staff dressed as police officers – though there's little authority about them; if anything they'll be partying along with you. Unpredictable (in the best sense), Jailhouse is the sort of place where Saturday night can be any night of the week and, almost, anything goes.

NEVER MIND BAR

Map 1; Nørre Voldgade 2, Indre By;

///forced.research.boldest; www.nevermindbar.dk

Never mind who you are or who you fancy, this city-centre stalwart will show you a good time. Come in the early hours: it's a final frontier post for young guns who keep the party going till dawn (don't be surprised if you end up at a house party after closing, too).

CAFÉ INTIME

Map 6; Allegade 25, Frederiksberg;

///lateral.fattest.panther; www.cafeintime.dk

Surrounded by tinted glass, naked flames and a grand piano, you'll feel like you're among creatives in 1920s Paris at Café Intime. This liberal bar has been welcoming LGBTQ+ folk since the early days (it was founded in 1922) and is beloved for its live music and drag shows.

» Don't leave without hitting the high notes at a sing-along evening. Every Wednesday, Café Intime invites the audience to take to the piano, strum an acoustic guitar and sing their hearts out.

COSY BAR

Map 1; Studiestræde 24, Indre By;

///respond.prepares.loudly; www.cosybar.dk

Every night at Cosy feels like a Eurovision party, with jovial groups of friends, fizzy drinks and a good old sing-along (no judgment here – even the tone deaf are encouraged to get involved). Get ready for chart toppers and bad dancing galore.

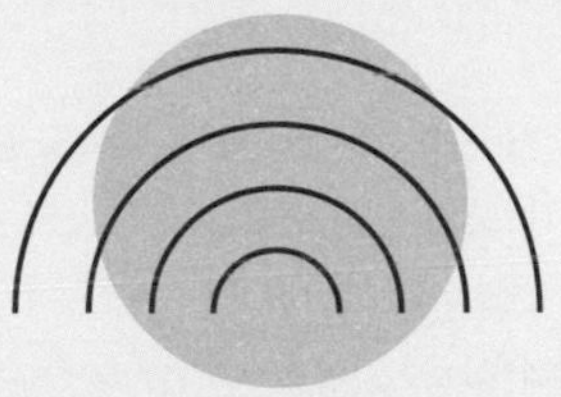

Liked by locals

"Not only will you find the world's oldest LGBTQ+ bar in the city centre, you'll also find that Copenhagen's nightlife is safe, inclusive, and easy to navigate, since many of the LGBTQ+ spots are located within walking distance."

AUGUSTO PELUSO, ACADEMIC RESEARCHER

Jazz Bars and Cafés

There are many things that change in Copenhagen, but the jazz scene – dating back to the 1920s – isn't one of them. Timeless candlelit cafés, good wine and the soft thud of a contrabass are never far away in this city.

LA FONTAINE

Map 1; Strædet 11, Indre By; ///tiger.slurs.boarding; www.lafontaine.dk

Looking for an expertly crafted evening of live jazz? Follow music bods and stylish young professionals to the city's oldest jazz bar. As a veritable cathedral of the genre, La Fontaine has witnessed some legendary performances and draws a solid crowd every night (be prepared, it can get cramped). Come during the Copenhagen Jazz Festival, in the summer months, to see the space at its most lively.

Try it!

EXPRESS YOURSELF

Your three minutes of fame start at the poetry club at La Fontaine. Sign up on the evening and join the nervous, the impassioned and the seasoned in free expression.

PALÆ

Map 4; Ny Adelgade 5, Indre By; ///valley.barks.scramble; www.palaebar.dk

Copenhagen's older, intellectual crowd have been coming to this informal spot for years, smoking under the dim lights, discussing politics and drinking no-nonsense beer. Join them (and a music-loving student crowd) to chew the fat and listen to the chilled jazz band that squeezes in here once a month.

JAZZHUS MONTMARTRE

Map 4; Store Regnegade 198A, Indre By; ///latched.verged.working; www.jazzhusmontmartre.dk

When jazz legends such as Dexter Gordon and Kenny Drew relocated to Copenhagen in the 60s (likely drawn by the Danes' appreciation for jazz), this cosy joint became their evening haunt. Now the venue prides itself on discovering a new generation of greats. Join attentive fans at the community tables and you might just catch the next Stan Getz.

CHRISTIANIA JAZZ CLUB

Map 5; Børneteateret, Psyak 61C, Christianshavn; ///bombard.modules.slumped; 51 50 55 39

Ashtrays and empty bottles lie scattered here and there, but don't judge – this spot may not put decor at the top of its priority list, but it does know how to put on a great jazz night. Expect the city's best musicians to slink in here after dark, with a cool crowd of locals hot on their tails.

» **Don't leave without** taking the stage at Christiania Jazz Club's Sunday jam sessions – they're open to the public.

Solo, Pair, Crowd

From concerts where the crowd don't utter a word to canalside music over a meal, there's jazz for all in this city.

FLYING SOLO

Join jazz bods

Tune in to an afternoon jam session while browsing records at Jazzcup. You'll be in the company of music fans doing the same as they leaf through the vinyl, nodding their heads to the record store's live jazz.

IN A PAIR

Canalside crooning

Located on Christianshavn's historic cobbled streets, Sofie Kælderen puts on memorable jazz concerts right by the canal. Keep an eye on its website for upcoming events.

FOR A CROWD

Party in Paradise

Got the Monday blues? Head to Paradise Jazz at Huset for an evening of big band. Expect a lively crowd dancing to the very best local and international acts. Bring your friends, get some drinks in and let's just pretend it's Friday.

CAFE HVIDE LAM

Map 1; Kulturovet 5, Indre By; ///rush.sheet.classics; 33 32 00 33

It's the crowd that shape a visit to this living-room-like spot. Old-timers sit at their favourite table, tapping their feet and savouring their daily jazz fix, while groups of office workers relax at the back with beers in hand, cheering on the band.

» Don't leave without staying for a beer after a jazz night has ended to hang out with the laidback crowd.

BEVAR'S

Map 3; Ravnsborggade 10B, Nørrebro; ///merchant.talents.zealous; www.bevars.dk

Bevar's is the type of place that stays buzzing all day and night. Students dash here in the morning, clutching their laptops and eager for coffee, while a relaxed crowd of young professionals saunter over in the evening. Wine freely flowing, they linger for the live jazz – which varies between up-beat bebop to easy listening, with the occasional experimental act thrown in for good measure.

CHARLIE SCOTT'S BAR

Map 1; Skindergade 43, Indre By; ///texted.clearing.examine; www.charliescotts.dk

Out-of-towners often discover this place by chance – either the cheers of football fans watching the game on the big screen or the sounds of a live jazz combo draws them in. Whichever takes your fancy, Charlie Scott's always promises a fun night.

0 metres 200
0 yards 200

Fill up at
BRUS

Prepare for the long night ahead with a carb-heavy meal (we recommend the vegetarian schnitzels), washed down with a beer from the on-site brewery.

Now indie cinema **Empire Bio**, *in 1991–2001 this spot housed a film studio run by legendary producer Kenneth Madsen.*

Get your groove on at
KASSEN

If you believe that a disco ball is essential to any party, then you'll love Kassen. Order a cocktail or mocktail before hitting the dance floor.

Catch a show at
SPILLESTEDET STENGADE

Get ready to dance like no one's watching at this temple-like concert hall. It's one of the city's best venues to see underground acts (think folk, reggae and everything in between).

Bring your A-game to
DUPONG

Join the locals for a game of table tennis at this bar. You'll be laughing and joking with your new-found friends in no time.

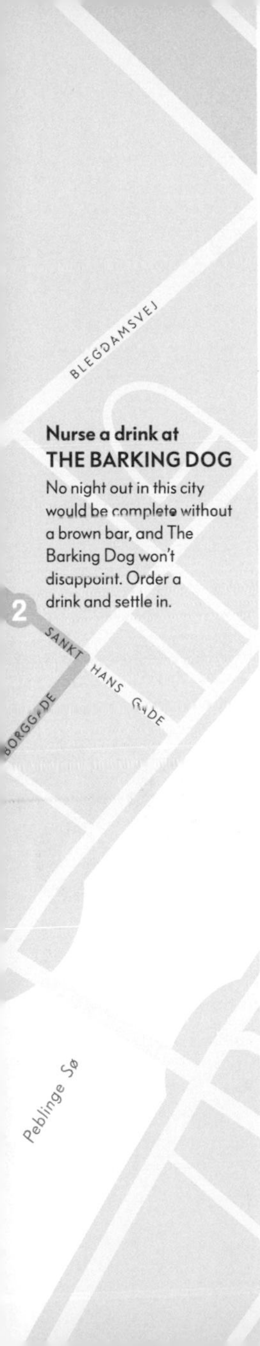

A night out in Nørrebro

By Copenhagen's standards, Nørrebro is a new neighbourhood. It emerged in the 1850s, when the city's growing working-class population burst out of the city walls. Immigrants and students chasing affordable housing soon followed, creating a buzzing, multicultural hub. Nights out in Nørrebronx (as it's affectionately known by its residents) are fuelled by cheap drinks, live music and conversations with new friends.

1. BRUS
Guldbergsgade 29F, Nørrebro; www.tapperietbrus.dk
///migrate.exacts.swan

2. The Barking Dog
Sankt Hans Gade 19, Nørrebro; www.thebarkingdog.dk
///stuffing.earlobe.reporter

3. Kassen
Nørrebrogade 18B, Nørrebro; www.kassen.dk
///gashes.this.cosmetic

4. Dupong
Griffenfeldsgade 52, Nørrebro; www.dupong.dk
///overnight.owls.someone

5. Spillestedet Stengade
Stengade 18, Nørrebro; www.stengade.dk
///crisps.pasting.spelling

Empire Bio
///radar.bikes.fairy

BLEGDAMSVEJ

Nurse a drink at THE BARKING DOG
No night out in this city would be complete without a brown bar, and The Barking Dog won't disappoint. Order a drink and settle in.

2

SANKT HANS GADE

BORGGADE

Peblinge Sø

OUTDOORS

Copenhageners are committed to protecting the natural world and spend as much time in it as possible. Whatever the weather, there's nothing better than a walk or swim.

Green Spaces

Copenhagen's parks aren't just open spaces. They're picnic spots, birthday hangouts and date venues. And every Copenhagener has a favourite green space where they go to feel closer to nature.

BOTANISK HAVE

Map 3; entrance via Gothersgade, Indre By; ///successes.artists.blasted; www.snm.ku.dk/botanisk-have

Okay, so much of this garden is indoors, within the vast and humid Palm House. But hear us out. While tourists make a beeline for the glinting greenhouse, Copenhageners pick up a cortado from the coffee cart, swerve the rockery and rhododendron garden, and hot-foot it to the lake. Here, they unroll picnic blankets and dip their feet in the water, while excited kids race around the lawn shrieking with glee.

FREDERIKSBERG HAVE

Map 6; entrance via Frederiksberg Allé, Frederiksberg; ///deaf.soothing.bats

Some Copenhageners might say that polished Frederiksberg isn't really Copenhagen. And they could be right – it isn't just a neighbourhood, Frederiksberg is its very own municipality. But that would be denying the city its "Green Village" and this pastoral expanse of rolling grass, dappled woodland and willow-kissed water. Things are quieter on weekdays, but come the weekend, it's a hive of activity – dog walkers stop to make conversation, joggers puff along the paths and groups walk off hearty brunches.

DET KONGELIGE DANSKE HAVESELSKABS HAVE

Map 6; entrance via Frederiksberg Allé, Frederiksberg; ///tree.gagging.movies

The tiny Royal Danish Horticultural Society's Garden is often mistaken for being part of Frederiksberg Have. But this oasis has a very different vibe to its neighbour. Here, the sounds of laughing kids, barking dogs and chatting walkers are replaced by the soothing soundtrack of water dripping daintily from fountains into shallow ponds. Relaxing, right?

ØRSTEDSPARKEN

Map 1; entrance via Nørre Voldgade, Indre By; ///fatter.brighter.wells

A hot contender for Copenhagen's loveliest picnic spot, Ørstedsparken envelops a lake that once formed a moat around the city. In summer, its green grass is dotted with gaggles of friends; in winter, bundled-up locals briskly circle the lake, clutching flasks of cocoa.

» **Don't leave without** picking up some picnic supplies from Torvehallerne market before hitting the park. You'll be spoilt for choice – stalls stock everything from pizza to porridge.

Solo, Pair, Crowd

Whether you're alone, in a duo or part of a group, there's a green adventure to fit every gathering.

FLYING SOLO

Bring a book

We know it sounds odd, but Assistens Kirkegård *(p112)* is ideal for a bit of R & R. Bring your book and lounge on the lawn, while author Hans Christian Andersen and philosopher Søren Kierkegaard lie at rest nearby. If you want to feel really meta, why not read one of their tomes?

IN A PAIR

A sheepish stroll

Alpacas and sheep might crash your date in Sydhavnstippen, but that's part of this park-cross-urban farm's charm. Take a stroll in the evening, when the light hits the water beyond the grass.

FOR A CROWD

Frisbee fun

Bring the gang, a frisbee and a picnic to Valbyparken for a fun-filled afternoon on the disc golf course.

KONGENS HAVE

Map 3; entrance via Gothersgade, Indre By; ///cheerful.racks.woke

Plonked in the middle of Indre By, the King's Garden is a much-needed slice of greenery. Come lunchtime, its paths are pounded by office workers plugged into their favourite podcasts. And on the weekend, something is always afoot in the manicured expanse of green, whether it's an alfresco concert, puppet show or birthday party.

LANDBOHØJSKOLENS HAVE

Map 2; entrance via Bülowsvej, Frederiksberg; ///outer.reviewed.audibly; www.landbohoejskolenshave.dk

Part of the University of Copenhagen's Faculty of Science, this flower-filled garden is a student fave. But don't go expecting a party vibe. On sunny days, students grab coffees from the greenhouse-turned-café, before settling on the grass to pour over library books for their next assignments. Join them on the lawn with a good paperback.

AMAGERFÆLLED

Map 5; entrance via Artillerivej, Amager; ///pony.paves.arrived

Amager Common is yet another example of Copenhagen's green ingenuity. What was once a landfill is now the city's greatest slice of wilderness. A rambling expanse of tousled meadows, windswept scrubland and dappled woodland, this is where city-dwellers go to get closer to nature.

» **Don't leave without** climbing Mount Anna. You'll soon prove the rumours about Copenhagen being flat wrong (hello, burning calves).

Wonderful Walks

For everyone from hardy hikers to Sunday strollers, weekends in Copenhagen are all about donning trainers, grabbing a takeaway coffee and striking out on a leisurely walk.

SØNDERMARKEN

Map 6; start at Pile Allé 53, Frederiksberg; ///shopping.screamed.invent

When Frederiksberg and Valby residents are seeking a lunchtime stroll, or need to clear their head after work, they hit this park's beech tree avenues, which pass fountains, pavilions and grottoes along the way. Expect to see the same faces (and dogs) here daily, politely nodding at one another as they pass by. Come autumn, the regulars are outnumbered as people flock here to see the fiery autumn leaves.

VESTRE KIRKEGÅRD

Map 6; start at Vestre Kirkegårds Allé 15, Vesterbro; ///goats.added.folk

Ambling through a graveyard may not be top of your to-do list, but the Western Cemetery is a good place for a catch-up – trust us. Conversation flows as you stroll under tree tunnels, with the

Join a free tour to learn more about the residents here. Tours run from April to September.

gravestones of the great and the good sparking endless interesting discussions (head to section A, where the most famous Danes can be found).

KALVEBOD FÆLLED

Map 6; start at Otto Baches Allé, Amager; ///dampen.folds.plotted

When the kids get antsy and need entertaining, parents make for this windswept common. Here, youngsters can let off steam while learning, as they spot mammals, amphibians and birds in the misty moorlands, dappled birch forests and tidal marches. Binocular-wielding wildlife watchers also stalk the paths, holing up in hides when they see something that piques their interest.

SØERNE

Map 3; start at Sortedams Dossering 101, Østerbro; ///labs.donates.snows

Skirting the sweeping lakes that bracket the city centre (known as Søerne), this waterside walk is the perfect way to soak up some city vibes. Wending your way from north to south, you'll hit up green Østerbro, where whistling dog walkers and puffing runners rule, artsy Nørrebro and hip Vesterbro. The hottest picnic spot en route? Dronning Louises Bro, hands down. During the summer months, this bridge is flooded with friends on makeshift picnic blankets, soaking up the waterfront views. Join them (if you can find a spot).

» **Don't leave without** grabbing a steaming brew from Den Franske Cafe on Sortedam Dossering.

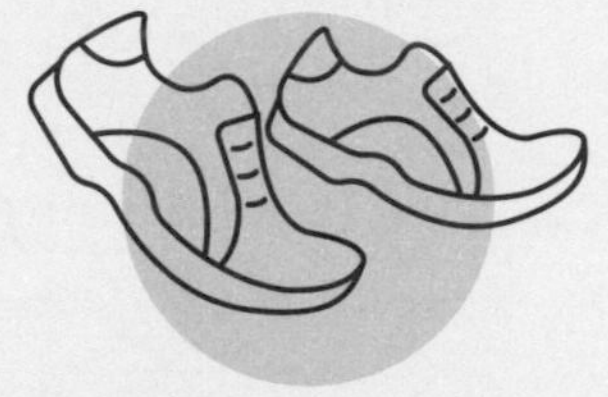

Liked by the locals

"Kastellet is all too often forgotten. In many ways, I like it like that. The fewer the number of people you encounter there, the deeper the feeling of going back to the past, leaving the chaos of the stressful streets."

EDOARDO BOTTALICO DOUGIE KEVIN, AVID WALKER AND LEAD SINGER OF EDWARD FOX & THE ANIMAL KINGDOM

KASTELLET

Map 4; start at Esplanaden 44, Østerbro; ///bonkers.watching.invite

Copenhagen's runners love pounding the trail that encircles Kastellet fortress (perhaps because its pentagonal shape instantly ups their step count). But why would you want to speed past these sea views? Take it slow, and soak up the sights.

HAVNEPARKEN

Map 5; start at Vestmannagade, Islands Brygge; ///arena.noticing.bugs

When the mercury starts to soar, the whole city seems to hit this waterfront park. And with its cooling sea breeze and summer sights, who can blame them? Groups of friends stroll along the vast promenade, pausing at Islands Brygge Harbour Bath before ducking into cute waterfront cafés.

» Don't leave without checking out the exhibition on Islands Brygge's history. It's held in a cool repurposed train carriage on the quayside.

STRANDVEJEN

Map 6; start at Charlottenlund Strandpark, Charlottenlund; ///catching.skin.scuba

Copenhagen may be full of walkable coastal suburbs but "Lunden", as it's affectionately known to the locals, was made for strolls – Sunday strolls, to be specific. With stunning views across the Øresund to Sweden, beautiful beaches peppered along the way and a straight route that doesn't require much thought or planning to follow, it's a no-brainer for a weekend wind-down.

City Squares

Copenhagen's squares have long been summertime meeting points, where people gather to watch royal weddings and sporting events, and to hang out with friends. Join the sun-loving locals at these spots.

LITAUENS PLADS

Map 2; entrance via Saxogade, Vesterbro; ///emphasis.donation.lavender

The considerate folk at Gottlieb Paludan Architects reimagined this historic square with the local community in mind. It's split into distinct areas: students make for the cobbled patch near the square's entrance on flea market days to browse; old boys play table tennis on the raised terrace; off-duty dads hit the basketball court; and friends while away summer evenings outside the café attached to Gethsemane Kirke. You could circle it five times and never tire of it all – it's authentic Vesterbro at its best.

SUPERKILEN PARK

Map 3; entrance at Nørrebrogade 210, Nørrebro; ///traffic.steams.unto

"Park" is a bit of a misnomer when it comes to Superkilen. Sure, it has a section of grass and trees but most of the area is made up of asphalt and concrete. Created by artist collective Superflex and the architects at Bjarke Ingels Group, Superkilen was designed to bring together Nørrebro's sometimes polarized community and we think it's succeeded. It's not one, but three interconnected spaces, with very different identities. The Red Square is a massive outdoor gym; The Black Market is an urban living room, with BBQ and backgammon facilities; and The Green Park is true to its name, with undulating hills and plenty of picnic areas.

» Don't leave without riding the swings in Den Røde Plads (The Red Square). They're a great way for adults to appreciate the playfulness of this square – children are very welcome to have a go, too.

BLÅGÅRDS PLADS

Map 3; entrance via Blågårdsgad, Nørrebro; ///punk.hands.dabbled

Formerly the site of a polluting iron foundry (earning the area the nickname "the Black Square"), Blågårds Plads is now a tree-lined public space right in the heart of Nørrebro. Something is always afoot here, be it a football game, alfresco music festival or winter ice-skating rink.

Try it!
TAKE A PARKOUR CLASS

Always wanted to try parkour, aka free running? Now's your chance. Street Movement runs pop-up beginners' classes every Wednesday at different squares in the city *(www.streetmovement.dk)*.

SANKT ANNÆ PLADS

Map 4; entrance at Bredgade 33, Indre By; ///recall.vague.ferrets

Many people pass through this square on their way to Ofelia Plads without giving it a second glance. But the embassy quarter's suit-clad office workers know to pause their lunch-break laps and take advantage of Sankt Annæ's manicured lawns, shady benches and swinging hammocks. Join them on this slice of green.

OFELIA PLADS

Map 4; entrance via Sankt Annæ Plads, Indre By; ///gashes.trading.wide

Located at the end of Sankt Annæ Plads, Ofelia Plads seems a world away from its strait-laced neighbour. Food trucks, live performances, art installations and pop-up events like yoga and dance classes give this square (well, it's actually more of a pier than a *plads*) a young and fun vibe.

Tucked away in the middle of new neighbourhood Carlsberg Byen is Thorvald Bindesbølls Plads, an oft-overlooked square. Once the forecourt of Carlsberg's bottling factory (now a cultural centre), it's been turned into a community space with a sunken football ground, woodland-style seating area and manicured shrubs. Rock up in the evening and join the residents of Carlsberg Byen's swanky condos (think bespectacled creatives and young families) for an impromptu game of footie on the pitch. Two left feet? Just watch.

GRÅBRØDRETORV

Map 1; entrance via Niels Hemmingsens Gade, Indre By; ///organs.square.garages

With a story dating back to 1238, Gråbrødretorv gives off major history book vibes. A wander through this cobblestone square is like walking along a timeline: pass the site of a 17th-century "pillar of shame" that people used to spit at to show their displeasure for disgraced politician Corfitz Ulfeldt; peek into colourful gabled houses that survived both the 1728 fire and bombardment by the British during the 1807 Battle of Copenhagen; and listen to alfresco performances during the Copenhagen Jazz Festival, which has been held in the square each July since 1979.

» **Don't leave without** taking a detour to Strøget to hear the shrill cry of the Sanger Søren, a falsetto busker who has a cult-like following.

ENGHAVE PLADS

Map 2; entrance via Istedgade, Vesterbro; ///fraction.coverage.maternal

Crisscrossed by tram lines from the early 20th century and home to a metro station since 2011, you'd be forgiven for thinking that Enghave Plads was just a transport hub. But this square, located at the end of Istedgade, has heart. It's a social hub on weekends, with skateboarders testing each other on the ramps, locals socializing on the red benches and children splashing about in the fountain. It's not all play though; locals put up such a strong fight when Copenhagen Metro tried to fell the square's 114-year-old tree that the company promised to plant a new one as a result. No surprise then that the area coined the slogan "Istedgade will never surrender". Talk about community spirit.

On the Water

Laced with canals and surrounded by the sea, this city is shaped by water and so too are Copenhageners' weekends. From high-octane kitesurfing to soothing waterside yoga, there's something for everyone.

KAYAK POLO

Map 5; Islands Brygge 18, Islands Brygge; ///tonsils.reflect.shine; www.bryggens-kajakpolo.dk

Ever played kayak polo? You're probably in the majority if your answer is no. Though it more closely resembles handball (a religion rather than a sport for some Danes), someone decided polo had a much better ring to it. Bring your squad and try not to capsize as you attempt to toss the ball into your opponents' goal, while stopping them from doing the same to you.

GREENKAYAK

Map 5; Børskaj 12, Indre By; ///feathers.audio.glitz; www.kayakrepublic.dk

Stunning city views reward those brave enough to paddle Indre By's canals, dodging tour boats on the way. If you're looking for a cheap way to do it, check out GreenKayak. It's free (you read right) to rent a kayak but there's a rather wonderful catch: you'll be picking up as much rubbish as you can while you paddle. What could be better than travelling under your own steam and making the place a little greener as you go?

» Don't leave without looking out for the Church of our Saviour's spiralling tower peeking out above the colourful façades as you navigate Christianshavns Kanal.

DFDS CANAL TOUR

Map 4; Nyhavn, Indre By; ///sketch.kings.jump; www.dfds.com

Parents in town? In-laws visiting? Book on a guided canal tour from Nyhavn and Gammel Strand and you've got the day sorted. We won't lie, these boats are popular with out-of-towners, but even long-time locals love learning new facts about their city once in a while. If you're looking for a sophisticated date night, join an evening jazz tour or a dinner cruise.

STAND-UP PADDLEBOARDING

Map 6; Svaneknoppen 1, Østerbro; ///mediate.crush.lodge; www.nauticeasy.com

Combining exercise with socializing, stand-up paddleboarding (SUP to the initiated) has Copenhageners falling hard and fast – literally. You can try it all over the city but water-sports school Nauticeasy is one of the most popular choices. Classes for beginners (and advanced courses for those experts among us) make it easy to pick up, leaving more time to admire the views as you navigate the water. Nauticeasy even runs yoga SUP classes for those who really want to bliss out.

Solo, Pair, Crowd

If the typical modes of transport don't float your boat, there are plenty of other options to enjoy the waters on.

FLYING SOLO

Feel the need for speed?

Take a leap of faith, fasten your seatbelt and prepare to be thrown across the waves at over 100 km/h (60 mph) with a group of screaming strangers on a RibAlex speedboat tour.

IN A PAIR

Pedalo for two

Rent a pedalo from Kaffesalonen and take to the Søerne lakes with your favourite friend. Some of the pedalos are shaped like swans, so you'll blend in perfectly with the local wildlife.

FOR A CROWD

Rent a hot tub

When it's minus something outside, and you're not one for winter bathing, a floating Copenhot tub is just what the doctor ordered. Pick up your group and relax in the warm waters – you're sure to be the envy of all the swimmers.

MOSEHOLM YOGA

Map 2; Ofelia Plads; ///just.breezes.device; moseholmyoga.com

As the sun rises, yogis grab their mats and cycle to Ofelia Plads *(p174)* for a morning class by the water. After mastering their downward dog positions, they'll usually take a cooling dip in the harbour, too – talk about the perfect detox.

» **Don't leave without** taking a picture of the view from your yoga mat: you'll see the famous Amalienborg Palace and the Opera House.

AMAGER KITESKOLE

Map 6; Amager Strandvej 130N, Amager; ///thing.melon.implore; www.amagerkiteskole.dk

Be it a breeze, a gust or even a gale, the wind is a constant companion in Denmark. So, when office workers need a bit of a break, nothing blows the cobwebs away quite like a kitesurfing lesson. Join them at one of Amager Kite School's taster sessions, which take place just off the coast at Sydvestpynten.

GO BOAT

Map 5; Islands Brygge 10, Islands Brygge; ///shocking.both.boarding; goboat.dk/en/

When the weekend hits and the sun starts to peek out, friends head to Islands Brygge to hire a solar-powered vessel for the day. Armed with a picnic, they sail around the city's waterways, enjoying the sights, drinking local wine and singing a little too loudly. A floating party to usher in the summer? Sign us up.

Swimming Spots

Whatever the weather, hardy Copenhageners can usually be found taking a dip in the city's harbours and canals. So, stop moaning about the cold, don your kit and wade in.

BELLEVUE STRAND

Map 6; Strandvejen 340, Klampenborg; ///dawn.aside.happily

During the winter, Bellevue's a quiet slice of coast frequented by brisk walkers and only the most devoted of swimmers. Come summer, every family in Copenhagen's northern suburbs hot-foots it here. Excited kids splash about in the gentle surf, friends set up volleyball games on the sand and parents sunbathe on beach towels.

» **Don't leave without** taking a picture of the blue-and-white lifeguard towers. These beauties were designed by Arne Jacobsen in 1932 and look like something straight out of a Wes Anderson film.

SLUSEHOLMEN

Map 6; Sydhavnen; ///costumes.burn.believer; www.sluseholmen.dk

Locals will tell you Sluseholmen is Copenhagen's version of Venice (though the water here is a lot cleaner). A former industrial dockland, this area is now an enviable place to live, with modern apartments overlooking a network of canals. Swimming spots are dotted along the waterways and, as this district is slightly off the beaten track, they're still a bit of a secret, too.

KALVEBOD BØLGE

Map 5; Kalvebod Brygge, Kalvebod Brygge; ///snake.flag.recount

Kalvebod Wave is made up of several undulating wooden platforms that span the harbour. It's essentially a playground over the water and Copenhagen's active locals can't get enough of it. There's always something going on here, whether it's parkour kids (with their stereos blasting out music) jumping between the structure's different levels or kayakers sliding down the ramp into the water. As for the swimmers, winter bathers often slink in from the lower levels while teenagers leap off the higher platforms in the summer.

SØNDRE REFSHALEBASSIN

Map 4; Refshaleøen; ///every.emerald.half

Home to students, start-ups and super-cool coffee shops, Refshaleøen is also a great spot for a swim. The harbour's quiet around here, so there's always plenty of space for a laidback dip. And sure, the view of the city's nothing to write home about, but the colourful, floating shipping containers (home to lucky students) provide pretty good eye candy instead. On sunny evenings and weekends, the place becomes a lot more buzzy, with students spilling out onto the harbour, their feet dangling over the edge and a beer bottle in hand.

AMAGER STRANDPARK

Map 6; Amager Strand Promenaden 1, Amager; ///fuel.horn.presume

On days when it's too hot to do anything else but swim, and the city centre spots don't quite cut it, sweltering urbanites slip on their flip-flops, pack a picnic and take the 12-minute train to this vast stretch of sand. Surrounded by cute shops and lively cafés, it's the perfect place to spend a sunny afternoon – and most of Copenhagen knows it.

» **Don't leave without** taking a pre-beach swim at the nearby Kastrup Sea Bath – known as "the snail" thanks to its curvaceous shape.

SANDKAJ

Map 6; Sandkaj 27, Nordhavn; ///entrust.giggle.dabbing

A community of thick-skinned regulars swim here through the winter but, for more sensitive souls, it's the first signs of summer that put this harbour bath on the map. Sun-worshippers bag a spot on the modern pier while office workers take a post-work dip in the water. Having worked up an appetite, they make a beeline for one of the nearby restaurants as soon as the sun drops below the horizon.

HAVNEVIGEN

Map 5; Vilhelm Buhls Gade, Islands Brygge; ///gripes.belonged.seating

This manicured bathing area isn't on most peoples' radar, so the young professionals who live around here usually have it all to themselves; some even have terraces that lead straight into the water, perfect for a quick dip. After a swim, the artificial beach is ideal for a leisurely sunbathe; you'll soon realize fake sand is just as good as the real stuff.

Liked by the locals

"If you're up for a winter dip, run for a short while before sinking into the water to warm your muscles up. Then, immerse yourself in stages, and make sure you've got company. Some of my favourite spots outside the city are Gilleleje port, Espergærde and Humlebæk."

HELENE RØMER EHRHARDT, YEAR-ROUND SWIMMER

Nearby Getaways

Of course Copenhageners love their city but sometimes a change of scene and gulp of fresh air is just the ticket. Luckily the city has various tempting day trips right on its doorstep.

MALMÖ

45 -minute train ride from Copenhagen Central Station;

www.visitsweden.com

Sweden's design capital is a just a hop, skip and jump (and a train ride) away from Copenhagen, making it the ideal spot for a Swedish sojourn. On the weekend agenda? A wander around the brightly coloured medieval old town (Gamla Staden) and the ultra-modern district of Västra Hamnen with its neo-futuristic "Turning Torso" building. There's also the epic drama of the Øresund Bridge (star of the hit Danish-Swedish TV series *The Bridge*) and the indie retail hot spot the Form/Design Center. Bonus point: it's cheaper to shop here than back in Denmark.

HELSINGØR

50-minute train ride from Copenhagen Central Station; www.helsingborg-helsingor.com

History-loving parents coming to town? This charming city is worth a trip. First off, there's the castle. Not only is Kronborg Slot a beautiful Renaissance building, it also inspired Shakespeare's Elsinore (Hamlet's home). Then there's the M/S Maritime Museum of Denmark, which covers Danes' seafaring prowess from the Vikings to today. But many Copenhageners skip these sights entirely. After all, there are markets to visit, smørrebrød to sample and fresh fish feasts. Why not make a weekend of it?

» **Don't leave without** hopping from stall to stall in Værftets Madmarked – Helsingør's indoor street food market. Come hungry.

UTTERSLEV MOSE

40-minute bus ride from Nørreport Station

Sprawling across the most northwestern edge of Copenhagen, this vast marshland feels worlds away from the hubbub of the city. Come the weekend, those craving the great outdoors take to the saddle and set off on an epic cycling adventure along its winding trails.

JÆGERSBORG DYREHAVE

20-minute train ride from Copenhagen Central Station; eng.naturstyrelsen.dk

Picture this: lush forests and large plains as far as the eye can see. Welcome to Jægersborg Dyrehave, Copenhagen's historic deer park. This is the day trip Copenhageners roll out when they want to get out into nature – for a gentle stroll with the in-laws or an adrenaline-fuelled BMX session with the gang. Dyrehaven never disappoints.

GENTOFTE

30-minute train ride from Copenhagen Central Station; www.gentofte.dk

Stressed-out office workers descend on Gentofte on their days off. And who can blame them? This quaint town in the northern suburbs of the capital is pure charm, with its tranquil lake, grand houses and tree-lined boulevards. Lovely stuff.

» **Don't leave without** catching a film at Gentofte Kino. This rustic, arthouse cinema has been screening movies since 1938.

FURESØ

1-hour train ride from Copenhagen Central Station; www.furesoe.dk

As soon as summer hits the region, Scandinavians have only one thing in mind: a lakeside retreat. And Furesø, Denmark's deepest lake, is hard to resist. Spending time here feels like a holiday: families, friends and couples while away days sunbathing on the sandy beaches, canoeing on the calm waters and, when the sun sets, roasting marshmallows by the fire.

ROSKILDE

20-minute train ride from Copenhagen Central Station; www.visitroskilde.com

Hippies came to Roskilde in the 70s for its huge music festival (Denmark's answer to Glastonbury), but these days it's a hipster heartland. Day-trippers come to browse the flea markets, catch some live music (yes, even outside festival season) and check out RAGNAROCK, a museum of pop, rock and youth culture.

HILLERØD

45-minute train ride from the Copenhagen Central Station; www.hillerod.dk

Escaping the city has always been the main reason to visit this royal suburb: once for the upper classes, now for all walks of life. Frederiksborg Slot undoubtedly hogs the headlines, given that it's Scandinavia's largest Renaissance palace. But most locals give it, and its manicured gardens, a wide berth, rather donning their walking boots and heading to Gribskov, a vast, untamed forest.

Try it!
FORAGE FOR FOOD

Developed by NOMA founder René Redzepi, the Vild Mad app helps identify edible plants, berries and fungi *(www.vildmad.dk)*. After foraging ingredients in Gribskov, follow one of the New Nordic recipes.

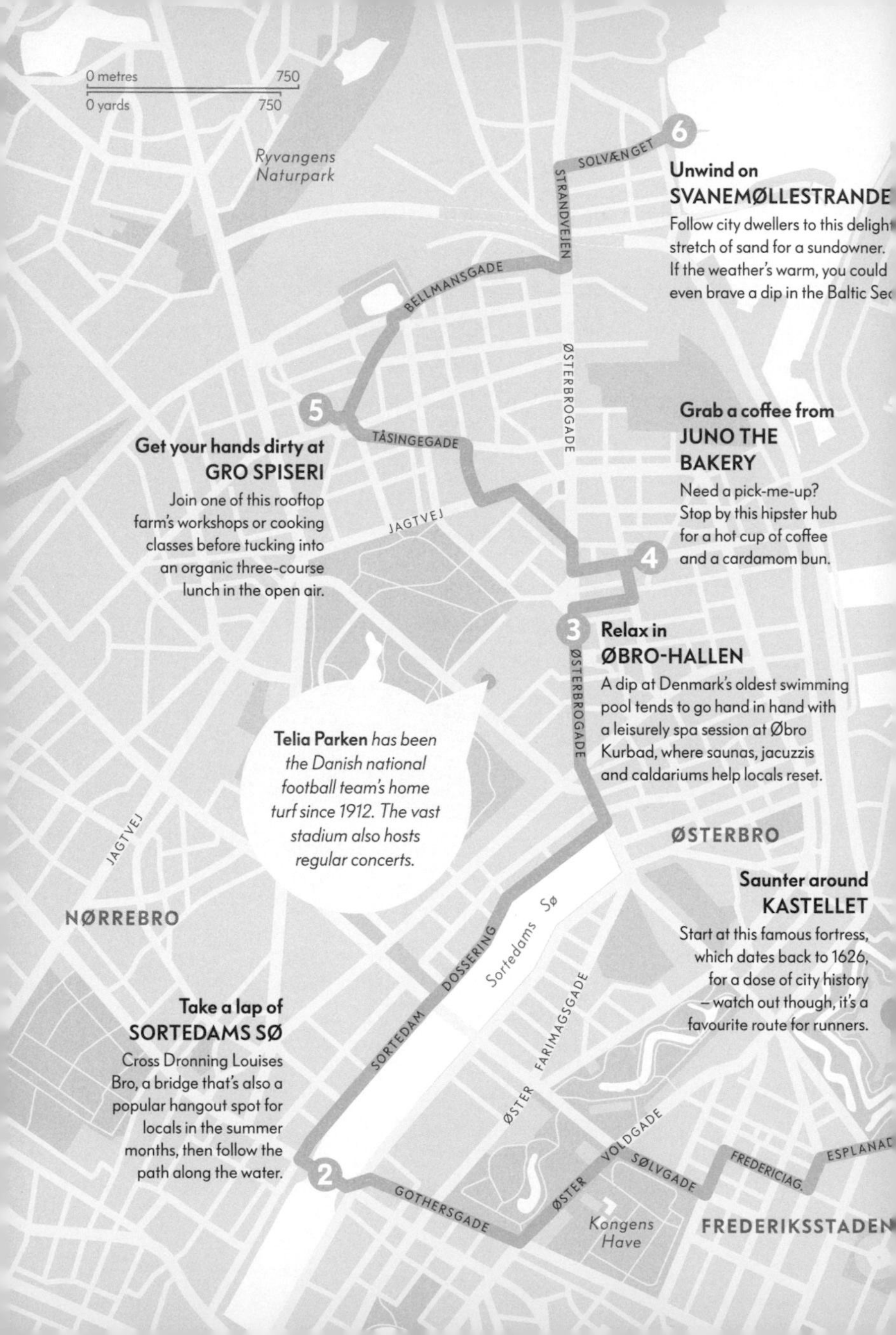

0 metres 750
0 yards 750

Ryvangens Naturpark

SOLVÆNGET

STRANDVEJEN

6

Unwind on
SVANEMØLLESTRANDE

Follow city dwellers to this deligh stretch of sand for a sundowner. If the weather's warm, you could even brave a dip in the Baltic Sea

BELLMANSGADE

ØSTERBROGADE

5

TÅSINGEGADE

Get your hands dirty at
GRO SPISERI

Join one of this rooftop farm's workshops or cooking classes before tucking into an organic three-course lunch in the open air.

Grab a coffee from
JUNO THE BAKERY

Need a pick-me-up? Stop by this hipster hub for a hot cup of coffee and a cardamom bun.

JAGTVEJ

4

3

Relax in
ØBRO-HALLEN

A dip at Denmark's oldest swimming pool tends to go hand in hand with a leisurely spa session at Øbro Kurbad, where saunas, jacuzzis and caldariums help locals reset.

ØSTERBROGADE

Telia Parken *has been the Danish national football team's home turf since 1912. The vast stadium also hosts regular concerts.*

JAGTVEJ

ØSTERBRO

Saunter around
KASTELLET

Start at this famous fortress, which dates back to 1626, for a dose of city history – watch out though, it's a favourite route for runners.

NØRREBRO

Sortedams Sø

SORTEDAM DOSSERING

ØSTER FARIMAGSGADE

Take a lap of
SORTEDAMS SØ

Cross Dronning Louises Bro, a bridge that's also a popular hangout spot for locals in the summer months, then follow the path along the water.

2

GOTHERSGADE

ØSTER VOLDGADE

SØLVGADE

FREDERICIAG.

ESPLANAD

Kongens Have

FREDERIKSSTADEN

A day out in idyllic Østerbro

Østerbro has it all: sparkling lakes, top-notch restaurants and sandy beaches. This verdant borough slowly transitions from the inner city to the seaside, making you feel like you've escaped the hustle and bustle of the centre without travelling too far at all. Stretch your legs in the area's many parks, grab a bite to eat in one of the beloved neighbourhood cafés or simply do as many a Copenhagener does in the summertime – laze around on the beach.

The statue of Hans Christian Andersen's **Little Mermaid**, *designed by Edvard Eriksen, has sat on these shores since 1913.*

1. Kastellet
Østerbro
///bonkers.watching.invite

2. Sortedams Sø
Østerbro
///timidly.fragments.held

3. Øbro-Hallen
Gunnar Nu Hansens Plads 3, Østerbro; www.svoemkbh.kk.dk
///secretly.sport.legs

4. Juno the Bakery
Århusgade 48, Østerbro
///struts.bottled.regulate

5. Gro Spiseri
Æbeløgade 4, Østerbro; www.grospiseri.dk
///harps.monopoly.shark

6. Svanemøllestranden
Østerbro
///tenses.sulked.jokes

Telia Parken *///edges.workshop.darker*

The Little Mermaid *///luring.ignoring.wipes*

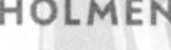

With a little research and preparation, this city will feel like a home away from home. Check out these websites to ensure a healthy, safe stay in Copenhagen.

Copenhagen

DIRECTORY

SAFE SPACES

Copenhagen is an inclusive city, but should you feel uneasy at any point or want to find your community, there are spaces catering to different genders, sexualities, demographics and religions.

www.boessehuset.dk

A welcoming centre for the LGBTQ+ community to come together for parties, theatre and other events.

www.femimam.com

Muslim mosque led by Denmark's first female imams. Friday prayer is for women only, but anyone can pray here at other times.

www.lgbt.dk

Organization running events and offering support for Denmark's LGBTQ+ community.

www.mosaiske.dk

Jewish community centre with information on synagogues, a kosher guide to the city and a hospitality group of local Jewish families that host visitors on Shabbat.

HEALTH

While healthcare in Denmark is free for its citizens and residents, comprehensive health insurance is essential for visitors. Emergency healthcare is covered by the European Health Insurance Card (EHIC) for EU residents and the UK Global Health Insurance Card (GHIC) for those from the UK. If you do need medical assistance, there are many pharmacies and hospitals.

www.apoteket.dk

The website of the Danish Pharmacists' Association lists pharmacies across the city and runs an online dispensary.

www. bispebjerghospital.dk
Bispebjerg Hospital operates an STD clinic in the centre of the city.

www.laegevagten.dk
Lists 24-hour pharmacies and provides night-time medical advice and care for situations not requiring an ambulance.

www.odontology.ku.dk
The Copenhagen School of Dentistry offers affordable dental treatment.

TRAVEL SAFETY ADVICE

Copenhagen is generally a safe city. Before you travel – and while you're here – always keep tabs on the latest regulations in Denmark.

en.coronasmitte.dk
The official Danish government website is the first port of call for all COVID-19 rules and regulations.

www.politi.dk/en
Denmark's police website, including news on major police incidents and information on how to report various crimes.

www.um.dk/en
Latest travel safety information, and up-to-date COVID-19 news and advice, from Denmark's Ministry of Foreign Affairs.

www.visitcopenhagen.com
Inspirational and practical information from the city's official tourism board.

ACCESSIBILITY

Copenhagen is ranked as one of Europe's most accessible cities for anyone with mobility concerns. These resources will help make your journeys go smoothly.

www.accessdenmark.com
A list of accessible businesses.

www.cph.dk/en/practical/travelers-with-diabilites
Information and assistance for navigating Copenhagen Airport.

www.kk.dk/toiletter
Lists and maps accessible public toilets throughout the city.

www.taxa.dk/en
Accessible taxi services, with ramps and lifts available (see also Dantaxi).

www.visitcopenhagen.com/copenhagen/planning/accessible-copenhagen-guide-disabled-travelers
A comprehensive list of venues, restaurants, attractions and travel bodies that are accessible to all.

ABOUT THE ILLUSTRATOR

Mantas Tumosa

Creative designer and illustrator Mantas moved from his home country of Lithuania to London back in 2011. By day, he's busy creating bold, minimalistic illustrations that tell a story – such as the gorgeous cover of this book. By night, he's dreaming of adventures away, catching up on the basketball and cooking Italian food (which he can't get enough of).

This book was made with Forest Stewardship Council™ certified paper – one small step in DK's commitment to a sustainable future. For more information go to www.dk.com/our-green-pledge

A NOTE FROM DK EYEWITNESS

The world is fast-changing and it's keeping us folk at DK Eyewitness on our toes. We've worked hard to ensure that this edition of Copenhagen Like a Local is up-to-date and reflects today's favourite places but we know that standards shift, venues close and new ones pop up in their place. So, if you notice something has closed, we've got something wrong or left something out, we want to hear about it. Please drop us a line at travelguides@dk.com

Main Contributors Allan Mutuku Kortbæk, Monica Steffensen
Senior Editor Lucy Richards
Senior Designer Tania Gomes
Project Editor Rebecca Flynn
Project Art Editor Bandana Paul
Editor Lucy Sara-Kelly
Proofreader Stephanie Smith
Senior Cartographic Editor Casper Morris
Cartography Manager Suresh Kumar
Cartographer Ashif
Jacket Designer Tania Gomes
Jacket Illustrator Mantas Tumosa
Senior Production Editor Jason Little
Senior Production Controller Stephanie McConnell
Managing Editor Hollie Teague
Managing Art Editor Bess Daly
Art Director Maxine Pedliham
Publishing Director Georgina Dee

First edition 2022

Published in Great Britain by Dorling Kindersley Limited, DK, One Embassy Gardens, 8 Viaduct Gardens, London SW11 7BW.

The authorised representative in the EEA is Dorling Kindersley Verlag GmbH. Arnulfstr. 124, 80636 Munich, Germany.

Published in the United States by DK Publishing, 1450 Broadway, Suite 801, New York, NY 10018.

22 23 24 25 10 9 8 7 6 5 4 3 2 1

A CIP catalog record for this book is available from the British Library.

A catalog record for this book is available from the Library of Congress.

ISSN: 1542 1554
ISBN: 978 0 2415 2387 2

Printed and bound in China.

www.dk.com